Etiquette Guide to Japan

Know the Rules
that Make the Difference

Boye De Mente is an acknowledged authority on the Orient and the author of more than 30 books. *Etiquette Guide to Japan* is his fourth in the Japan Quick-Guide series. He first came to Japan in 1949 with the U.S. Army Security Agency and has been involved with Japan as a journalist, editor, lecturer, and writer ever since.

Etiquette Guide to Japan

Know the Rules
that Make the Difference

by

Boye Lafayette De Mente

TUTTLE PUBLISHING
Boston • Rutland, Vermont • Tokyo

Published by Tuttle Publishing
an imprint of Periplus Editions (HK) Ltd.

LCC Card No. 89-51722
ISBN 0-8048-3417-2

First printing, 1990
Ninth printing, 2001

Printed in Singapore

Distributed by:

Japan & Korea
Tuttle Publishing
RK Building 2nd Floor
2-13-10 Shimo-Meguro
Meguro-ku, Tokyo 153 0064
Tel: (03) 5437 0171
Fax: (03) 5437 0755

North America
Tuttle Publishing
Distribution Center
Airport Industrial Park
364 Innovation Drive
North Clarendon, VT 05759-9436
Tel: (802) 773 8930
Fax: (802) 773 6993

Asia-Pacific
Berkeley Books Pte. Ltd.
5 Little Road, #08-01
Singapore 536983
Tel: (65) 280 1330
Fax: (65) 280 6290

Contents

Preface   9

Note on Pronunciation   12

1
Origins of Japanese Etiquette   15
2
The Vertical Society   17
3
The Role of Harmony   19
4
The Language of Etiquette   21
5
The Use of Names   23
6
The Use of Titles   27

Contents

7
Introductions and Relationships   30

8
Exchanging Name Cards   34

9
Bowing   39

10
Shaking Hands Japanese-Style   43

11
Seating   45

12
Dining Etiquette   47

13
The Japanese Way of Drinking   51

14
Paying the Bill   55

15
Public Etiquette   57

16
Public Transportation   61

17
Bathing   64

Contents

18
Gift-Giving   68

19
Home-Visiting Etiquette   73

20
Praise   78

21
Criticism   80

22
The Tea Ceremony   83

23
The Apology   90

24
Appreciation   92

25
Dating   95

26
Weddings   99

27
Funerals   103

28
Attending a Wake   107

Contents

29

Attending a Funeral Service   109

30

Temples and Shrines   111

31

Obfuscation   113

32

Inns   115

33

Saying Farewell   118

Glossary of Etiquette Terms   123

Preface

Etiquette is defined as a body of prescribed social usages or, in more common terms, as a code of conduct describing behavior expected of members of a particular society in various situations. Obviously there could not be much of a society if members had no rules of conduct, but the type of behavior expected varies widely from one society to another. As is well known, behavior that might be the epitome of courtesy in one country may be regarded as a gross insult in another country.

The etiquette of a country also goes a long way toward defining its national character and the image of its people in the eyes of the rest of the world. But this image is always incomplete and often incorrect. A highly stylized, formal etiquette may be the product of a primitive or an advanced civilization and may have little or no correlation with the impulse to humanistic or intelligent behavior.

Japan is an example of a country in which the code of social conduct became so formal, so detailed, and so important that proper behavior became the paramount law of the land, regularly taking precedence over human feelings and ethical considerations. Yet it was combined with a reverence for nature and an acute awareness of the sensual and spiritual side of life that tempered some of its harsher realities.

For generations, the ethical and moral standards of the Japanese were measured in terms of their knowledge of and adherence to a minutely detailed, highly stylized etiquette. There was a prescribed form and order for virtually every action, from routine daily tasks to special occasions. Failure to follow the established forms of behavior was regarded as a transgression against the family, the community, and even the nation.

The Japanese were certainly not the first people to create a social system based on a highly stylized form of behavior, but there have been few, if any, societies that have carried the stylization as far as have the Japanese, or have made adherence to prescribed social norms such an integral part of the popular culture.

Japanese culture has changed significantly in recent decades, particularly since 1945, when personal freedom was introduced into the family and political systems. But enough of the traditional etiquette remains to set the Japanese apart socially and psychologically, and to make success in socializing and doing business with them a special challenge.

Fortunately the Japanese are well aware that the subtleties, complexities, and rigid formalities of their etiquette system are not easily learned or followed by outsiders. Thus, generous allowances are made for them. Nonetheless, it is very important for visitors to Japan to know something about Japanese etiquette. Firstly, it helps them avoid serious social transgressions and interact more successfully with the Japanese. Secondly, it allows them to participate in unique cultural rituals that are sensually, intellectually, and spiritually satisfying.

Note on Pronunciation

The six key sounds of Japanese are represented by the English letters *a, i, u, e, o,* and *n.* The five vowels are pronounced as follows:

a	as in f*a*ther
i	as in Bal*i*
u	as in tr*u*e
e	as in pr*e*ss
o	as in c*o*lt

These vowels and the *n* sound are "syllables" in themselves, and the vowels also combine with consonants to produce all the other syllables of Japanese. For example, the five vowel sounds plus the consonant *k* combine to produce *ka, ki, ku, ke,* and *ko,* pronounced "kah, kee, kuu, kay," and "koh."

Long vowels are pronounced twice as long as regular vowels and are marked *ā, ii, ū, ē,* and *ō.* Most syllables in Japanese are distinctly pronounced. At times, however, the *i* and *u* vowel sounds are weak, and the syllable is not clearly pronounced. Thus, the word *desu* be-

Date Due Receipt

Items checked out 04/03/2019 at

Bel Tib Library

thelibrary.info

comes "dess" and *yoroshiku* becomes "yoe-roshe-kuu."

In this book, Japanese words are first written with the modified Hepburn romanization system, with long vowels indicated by a macron. This is followed by the phonetic spelling used in the other Quick-Guides, a system readily understandable even by those encountering Japanese for the first time.

1

Origins of Japanese Etiquette

The primal impetus for the development of an etiquette-oriented culture in Japan no doubt originated in the native religion called Shinto, which translates as "way of the gods."

Shintoism was essentially a type of nature worship in which all things, including rivers, rocks, and trees, were considered to have spirits, to whom a degree of reverence was due. The focus of Japanese worship, however, was a pantheon of Shinto gods who controlled all the forces of nature as well as the welfare of the people.

Believing their world inhabited by innumerable spirits and gods, the Japanese developed a respectful attitude toward the seen as well as the unseen. This attitude was to shape their character from the beginning of their history and set the stage for the emergence of one of the world's most mannered societies.

According to the creation myth of Japan, Izanagi and Izanami, a god and goddess, gave birth to the Japanese islands. They were so enchanted with the beauty of their handiwork that they descended from the heavens to live on the islands. The story goes on to say that the Japanese themselves were the descendants of lesser gods who also settled on the island chain.

The lineage of Japan's earliest leaders, who combined the functions of high priest and sovereign, was traced directly to the divine ancestors in whose name they ruled. Thus, from the dawn of its history, Japanese society was structured according to religious tenets that required a very circumspect behavior and numerous formal ceremonies.

Another factor that was to play a crucial role in the development of etiquette in Japan was the sweeping importation beginning in the mid-sixth century of Korean and Chinese fashions, philosophies, and social customs.

By this time, China was already over three thousand years old and had a highly refined and stylized culture based on a concept familiar to the Japanese—a godlike emperor ruling over vassals and slaves and supported by a hierarchy of powerful underlings whose stations also entitled them to reverential treatment.

Japan borrowed extensively from China its writing system, styles and techniques of art and architecture, secrets of technology and medicine, and religious, philosophical, and legal systems. The heart of the Chinese etiquette system was the culture of the imperial court, and this became the model for the Japanese.

2

The Vertical Society

Just as in ancient China, early Japanese society was divided into distinct classes that were arranged in descending order of power and privilege. At the top of the pyramid was, of course, the emperor, followed by members of the royal family, court officials, priests, members of the military, scholars, artisans, farmers, and merchants.

The social system was a vertically arranged hierarchy of superiors and inferiors in which very specific kinds of behavior were required to demonstrate and maintain social differences and to cater to the vanity of those on higher levels.

As in most feudalistic societies, classes in Japan became hereditary and were eventually fixed by law. The phenomenon that most affected the behavior of all Japanese was the appearance and growth of a professional class of warriors in the twelfth and thirteenth centuries, who came to be known as samurai, from an old word meaning "to guard."

The government of the shoguns (essentially a military dictatorship), which first appeared in 1192, had its army of samurai warriors, as did each of the provincial clan lords around the country. The samurai, the only

17

citizens permitted to carry weapons and hold office, developed a lifestyle centered around the use of the sword, a total loyalty to their masters, and a system of formal etiquette that was prescribed down to the slightest bodily movement.

The samurai made Zen Buddhism their own special religion because of its strict advocacy of an extraordinary degree of mental and physical discipline. Constant training with swords and other weapons made the samurai, as a group, the most fearsome warriors in the world. Equally intensive training in the strictest etiquette also made the samurai the most mannered class of people in the world.

Common people of feudal Japan had few rights and were subject to the wishes and whims of the ruling samurai and their lords. Rural commoners were required to behave in a submissive and obedient manner toward their clan lords and the samurai retainers of their lords. Townspeople were expected to be equally subservient to the town magistrates and their samurai police.

The virtually absolute power of the samurai made many of them arrogant and only too willing to mete out swift punishment with their swords. Recourse to a higher authority was rare during most of Japan's long feudal age (1192–1868), with the result that the common people became extraordinarily passive and obedient.

So powerful was the presence of the samurai class that their style of living and their exquisitely choreographed etiquette became the role model for all Japan. Their influence was to color the entire cultural fabric, setting the standards that many Japanese today still strive to attain in many areas of their lives.

3

The Role of Harmony

Japan's first centralized government, dating from around 600 B.C. (according to unsubstantiated records), was based on the concept of *kōchi kōmin* (koe-chee koe-meen), in which all of the people literally belonged to the emperor, had no inherent freedoms, and could not own private property. This system lasted until the eighth century A.D.

The foundation for the social system during this long period was harmony, *wa* (wah). This was a hierarchical harmony that required each individual, regardless of his place in the vertical structure, to do exactly what was expected of him in the exact manner prescribed. The one absolute in the system was harmony—between men and the gods and among men—all within the context of the superior-inferior structure of the society.

In this system, all behavior and all relationships—personal, public, and professional—were controlled by a carefully prescribed etiquette that took precedence over human feelings as well as practical reasoning. Although the concept of *kōchi kōmin* had substantially weakened by the ninth century, the attitude and much of the behavior it spawned were to continue in Japan up to modern times.

To hear most older Japanese tell it, *wa* remains the basic building block of Japanese society and, therefore, is responsible for its economic success. Many Japanese cultural traits, including decision-making by consensus, groupism, shared responsibility—even resistance to foreign companies entering the Japanese market—are predicated on the need and desire for purely Japanese-style harmony.

Having been conditioned for centuries to a codified system of behavior that took on the color and force of a religion, the Japanese became so accustomed to "the Japanese way" that they developed an extreme sensitivity to any deviation. Unexpected or deviant behavior not only disrupted the cultural imperative of harmony, it was also extremely stressful.

Japanese today are still extraordinarily sensitive to non-Japanese behavior. This sensitivity and the ensuing stress are part of the reason for the general resistance to foreign companies and foreign workers coming into the country. Some Japanese become nervous wrecks after being exposed to Westerners for only a few hours.

Another important aspect of harmonized behavior was that it made life predictable. Japanese could anticipate attitudes and reactions of other Japanese to the point that verbal communication was often unnecessary.

The Japanese eventually came to pride themselves on their "telepathic" ability, pointing to it as one of the cultural characteristics that made them different from other people—and superior.

Since Japan's cultural telepathy is etiquette-based, it is generally not recognized or is incomprehensible to anyone not intimately familiar with Japanese behavior. Anyone, visitor or resident businessman, who wants to truly understand and communicate with the Japanese must therefore become intimate with their etiquette.

4

The Language of Etiquette

The importance of harmony and etiquette in the Japanese scheme of things had a profound effect on the development and use of the Japanese language. The sensitivity of the Japanese to superior-inferior relationships, to the imperative that they pay calculated respect and obsequiousness to superiors in word as well as deed, made them obsessively sensitive to language.

Over the centuries, special words, special word endings, and several different "levels" of the Japanese language emerged as part of the overall etiquette system. There developed special words and word endings for women only and for men only. There came to be a highly stylized language used at the imperial court; a lower level used at the court of the shogun and the provincial lords; a formal level used when addressing superiors; a style used in speechmaking, formal writing, and news reporting; a style used when addressing equals; a style used when addressing inferiors.

These larger categories of the Japanese language, which are still in use today, are sufficiently different so as to resemble dialects. Each "dialect" has its own vocabulary and style and requires substantial study and practice to master.

The average Japanese can understand most of the different categories of the language fairly well simply from exposure to them from childhood, but skill in using them does not come automatically.

In addition, special groups and classes of people, including Japan's gangsters, the *yakuza* (yah-kuu-zah), have their own special jargons. The residents of several regions have their own dialects. Some of these jargons and dialects are so different from standard Japanese that an outsider cannot understand them.

Another important aspect of language etiquette in Japan is the constant use of *aizuchi* (eye-zuu-chee), or what can be loosely translated as "agreement interjections." This refers to the Japanese custom of regularly and systematically agreeing with or acknowledging the comments of other persons by nodding one's head and/or saying such things as *hai* (high), *sō desu ka?* (soe dess kah), and *ah sō?* (ah soe) during the course of conversations.

These *aizuchi* interjections are expected and needed by the Japanese. If they are not forthcoming, the speaker knows immediately that something is wrong. He knows the other person is angry or disagrees with him to the extent that that person is deliberately breaking a sanctified custom. Japanese-speaking foreigners who are not familiar with the importance of *aizuchi* and who fail to follow through with the appropriate interjections may unwittingly send unintended messages.

All told, the role of the Japanese language in the etiquette system is central to proper behavior and is the key to getting "inside" the culture. Included in the back of this book are institutionalized Japanese words and phrases pertaining to various situations covered in the guide. By learning when and how to use them, one can greatly improve one's ability to communicate successfully with the Japanese.

5

The Use of Names

Two of the primary characteristics of the Japanese etiquette system are its formality and officialism. This has given rise to the custom of using last names in a formal manner in casual, even intimate, situations, and restricting the use of first names to very limited situations.

Parents address their children by their first names, and children and young people who are close friends will use first names among themselves, but adults who are unrelated habitually call each other by their last names no matter how long they may have been acquaintances or friends. Dating couples, however, now often use first names or, more correctly, diminutives of first names, which is a category in itself.

Many Japanese first names consist of two or more syllables awkward or bothersome to pronounce. This, plus the familiarity and intimacy factor among family and school friends, results in most first names being diminutized into the first syllable or the first two syllables plus *chan* (chahn), the familiar form of *san*. This is the Japanese equivalent of changing Robert to Bobbie, and Rebecca to Becky.

Chan is also used by parents and others to children; by children to their parents, grandparents, older brothers and sisters, and others who are close to them.

Some examples of commonly diminutized names follow:

Kiyoshi — *Ki-chan* (kee-chahn)
Yasunori — *Yasu-chan* or *Ya-chan* (yah-chahn)
Tomoko — *Tomo-chan* (toe-moe-chahn)
Minoru — *Mi-chan* (me-chahn)

Some examples of commonly diminutized titles include:

Father *(O-tō-san)* — *O-tō-chan* (oh-toe-chahn)
Mother *(Okā-san)* — *Okā-chan* (oh-kaah-chahn)
Grandmother *(Obā-san)* — *Obā-chan* (oh-baah-chahn)
Grandfather *(O-jii-san)* — *O-jii-chan* (oh-jeee-chahn)

Generally, Japanese husbands born before 1940 call their wives *o-mae* (oh-my) or *kimi* (kee-me), both forms of "you," or *okā-san* (oh-kaah-sahn), meaning "mother" or "mama." Men born during the 1940s and 1950s are likely to use some or all of the above terms, but those who have become more internationalized may also call their wives by their first names.

As a rule, wives born during the 1950s or earlier do not use their husbands' first names. They call them *anata* (ah-nah-tah), which in this usage means "dear," or *o-tō-san* (oh-toe-sahn), which translates as "father" or "papa."

It is now common for younger husbands and wives, particularly those born after 1960, to use first names in addressing each other. Once they have children, however, they are more likely to address each other as *okā-san* and *o-tō-san. San* is the Japanese equivalent of Mr., Mrs., or Miss, but in this usage it just adds politeness to the terms. When they become grandparents, couples use *obā-san* (oh-baah-sahn), "grandmother," and *o-jii-san* (oh-jee-sahn), "grandfather," to address each other.

Close school friends are expected to convert to the formality of last names once they finish school and go to work. Women who have known each other since grade school and remain close over the following years, will generally follow the same pattern and begin using last names after they marry and especially as they grow older.

While the use of names in Japan is being ever-so-slowly Americanized, and even though more and more Japanese are now beginning to gingerly use the first names of new and old foreign friends, it is still unthinkable for a middle-aged or older Japanese businessman to call a Japanese colleague by his first name, as Westerners commonly do.

Foreign visitors and businessmen should exercise caution in addressing older Japanese by their first names—unless they specifically ask that you do, or unless they have adopted a foreign first name and use it when introducing themselves to you. Those who have adopted a foreign name have done so specifically for use by their foreign friends and acquaintances.

However, even if a Japanese has a foreign first name, it is wise to use his last name in a business setting when other Japanese are present (unless they *all* have foreign first names or they specifically ask you to use their Japanese first names). Referring to just one Japanese in a group by a foreign first name would grate on the sensibilities of the others.

6

The Use of Titles

Another key factor in the
vertically arranged Japanese society is the importance
of using titles. Titles were used to rank people within
the hierarchy of their group as well as to designate the
classification or category of their work or profession.
Given the depersonalization of the individual in favor
of the group, titles tended to take on an entity of their
own and to take precedence over the individuals temporarily bearing them.

In feudalistic, martial Japan it became the custom
to refer to people by their titles instead of their names,
as is common in the military in all countries (and in Brit-
ish government circles). This exalted the title instead of
the individual and helped maintain the hierarchical relationship between the various classes and between the
categories of activity within those classes.

The butcher was *Nikuya-san* (nee-kuu-yah-sahn), or
"Mr. Meat Man." The carpenter was *Daiku-san* (die-
kuu-sahn), or "Mr. Carpenter." The warrior was
Samurai-san (sah-muu-rye-sahn), or "Mr. Samurai." The
guest was *O-kyaku-san* (oh-kyack-sahn), "Mr. Guest," or
O-kyaku-sama (oh-kyack-sah-mah), an even more polite
form of address.

The American use of the title accorded to the country's top political leader can be used to illustrate the Japanese system. The president is addressed as "Mr. President" in lieu of his name. In Japan all titles—those for government offices, company positions, professions, and even many mundane occupations—came to be used in a similar way.

In companies today, the chairman, presidents, general managers, managers, and section chiefs are generally referred to by title instead of name. Here are some examples of business titles:

chairman of the board — *kaichō* (kye-choe)
president — *shachō* (shah-choe)
vice-president — *fuku-shachō* (fuu-kuu-shah-choe)
senior (executive) managing director — *senmu* (sem-muu)
executive managing director — *jōmu* (joe-muu)
department manager (general manager)–*buchō* (buu-choe)
deputy general manager of the department—*buchō dairi** (buu-choe die-ree)
section manager — *kachō* (kah-choe)
deputy section manager — *kachō dairi* (kah-choe die-ree)
supervisor — *kakari-chō* (kah-kah-ree-choe)

*Only *dairi* is used when addressing deputy managers.

In public and private life the teacher or professor is
Sensei (sen-say-e); the doctor is *O-isha-san* (oh-ee-shah-
sahn), or "Mr. Doctor"; the taxi driver is *Unten-shu-san*
(uun-ten-shoe-sahn), or "Mr. Driver"; the single girl
is *O-jō-san* (oh-joe-sahn), or "Miss Young Lady"; the
married woman is *Oku-san* (oak-sahn), literally "Mrs.
Interior," really meaning "Mrs. Wife"; one's senior in
school or professional endeavor is *Senpai* (sen-pie), which
may be translated as "Senior" or "Elder." These titles
are commonly used in ordinary conversation in place
of the names of the individuals concerned.

Of course, it is not essential that the foreign visitor
or businessman in Japan conform to the custom of using titles instead of names. But by doing so you demonstrate knowledge and appreciation of Japanese customs
(which is appreciated in turn) and you communicate
more clearly because you are talking "their language."
There is also the personal satisfaction of doing things
the right way, plus the fact that using titles often allows
you to politely address someone directly and personally
without knowing their name (or avoid misusing it if you
can't pronounce it properly).

Other useful common titles:

train conductor —*shashō-san* (shah-show-sahn)
policeman —*o-mawari-san* (oh-mah-wah-ree-sahn)
school principal —*kōchō sensei* (koe-choe sen-say-e)
postman —*yūbin-ya-san* (yuu-bean-yah-sahn)
Prime Minister —*Sōri-daijin* (soe-ree-die-jeen)

Buddhist monk —*o-bō-san* (oh-boe-sahn)
Shinto priest —*kannushi-san* (kahn-nuu-she-sahn)
Catholic priest —*shimpu-san* (sheem-puu-sahn)
visitor/guest —*o-kyaku-sama* (oh-kyack-sah-mah)

7

Introductions and Relationships

Self or "cold" introductions were considered impolite and traditionally frowned on in Japan. Firstly, they required individuals to be aggressive (risking angering the other party). Secondly, the other party had no way of quickly verifying identities or claims. Thirdly, the party was always reluctant to take on new obligations, and fourthly, there was no mutually acquainted third party who could take responsibility for the new acquaintance.

This attitude toward self-introductions developed because the Japanese were group oriented, and groups tended to be exclusive and competitive. Rival groups were invariably suspicious of each other and it was difficult or impossible for a person to leave one group and become an accepted member of another group. Communication between groups was minimal and limited to formal, structured contact.

In this context, every stranger was an outsider who

was to be kept at a distance. This did not mean that strangers were treated impolitely; rather the politeness shown them acted as a barrier to becoming known and accepted and to establishing relationships with individual group members and, through them, with the group.

Because of the reluctance to establish new relationships—which would increase responsibility and the possibility of problems—the Japanese characteristically limited their close ties to members of their own groups. They became accustomed to accepting new people into the outer fringes of their circles only if the newcomers came to them with introductions from known and trusted contacts.

By the same token, if you were able to obtain an introduction through someone to whom the person you wished to meet was obligated—a professor, a doctor, an important supplier, or an official at a financial institution—that person would be under heavy obligation to meet you and do whatever he could for you.

This Japanese attitude toward self-introductions has been diluted since the trend to "going international" began in the 1960s, but it is still an important factor in establishing business contacts. The chances of being received with more than polite ceremony and of not being put off with very subtle rejections are greatly enhanced if one starts with an introduction from an individual or company the other party knows and respects.

If you must introduce yourself, you are advised not to ask for or expect any action to be taken on your behalf as a result of the first meeting. You must be able and willing to spend a considerable amount of time nurturing the relationship with personal visits, by eating and drinking together, and by gradually establishing the credibility and confidence necessary to be taken seriously.

However, if you are not Japanese and the situation is not business related, the reaction can be so positive it is startling and sometimes embarrassing. In this case, it is typical for the Japanese to treat you as a special guest, go out of their way to accommodate you, and extend overwhelming hospitality.

Such a positive reaction is partly due to the very strong but somewhat contradictory desire, in view of their normal group cohesion, the Japanese have to be liked and admired by foreigners. It is also due to the tendency on the part of the Japanese individual, who finds himself in the role of host, to feel that he personally represents the whole Japanese nation. It behooves him to make the best possible impression for fear that, if he does not, all Japan will lose face.

Another factor that sometimes misleads foreign businessmen is the generous amount of company money normally allotted Japanese managers to spend on clients and potential business contacts. It is common for many of them to royally entertain visitors because they themselves enjoy doing the town at someone else's expense— not because they foresee a potential business relationship. Not being able to "read" this kind of behavior, many foreigners delude themselves into thinking they have made a great impression.

In any first meeting with a Japanese, a key part of the introduction is identifying your company and professional relationship or your work status if you are self-employed, retired, etc.. If you are employed by a known company or are a member of a prestigious organization or profession, your chances of being well received are enhanced. The higher and more impressive-sounding your title, the more likely the Japanese will react to you positively.

Because of the structure and psychology of Japanese society and the formalities demanded by its etiquette, the Japanese generally cannot immediately develop close personal relationships with new acquaintances, particularly with people who are not on their social or company level. It is virtually impossible for them to develop close, informal ties with other Japanese of higher rank who have not been "de-Japanized" at least to some degree.

In fact, the Japanese are able to develop informal relationships with foreigners faster, and often more deeply, than they can with other Japanese, because the Japanese code of conduct does not strictly apply. At the same time, visitors should be very cautious about behaving informally with older Japanese who are senior in age and rank. Unless those Japanese individuals have developed an international attitude, they are likely to react negatively to informality.

In any event, it is wise to keep Japanese etiquette and the special sensitivities of the Japanese in mind when embarking on any relationship. It is also important to keep in mind that the ability of the Japanese to speak English is not always an accurate reflection of their degree of Westernization or comfort level with Western behavior. This is especially true of those who studied English only in Japan.

8

Exchanging Name Cards

Name cards are especially important in Japan, particularly in business situations. Their importance derives from the traditional vertically arranged social structure of feudal Japan. The prescribed etiquette for every individual was primarily determined by his or her clan, class, group affiliation, or position. Following the correct etiquette was critical—in some cases one's life depended on not making a serious error.

This system made it imperative for people meeting for the first time to identify each other's position in the social hierarchy quickly and accurately in order to determine which rules of etiquette applied. If no relationship was desired, strangers ignored each other—at a safe distance when possible, and with studied indifference when close contact was unavoidable. When a relationship was desired or was unavoidable, a mode of introduction that was appropriate to the stranger's rank and class was established.

Among ranking, higher-class people, introductions were very formal and stylized. Warriors, preparing for combat to the death, would often go through an elaborate ritual of self-introduction that would not have been out of place on a Shakespearean stage. Professional gamblers, in a parody of the upper classes and sword-carrying samurai, also devised lengthy, intricate styles of introducing themselves to rivals—and sometimes to the law.

Prior to the Meiji Restoration in 1868, class, rank, and group identity could often be determined by several visible factors, including apparel and family crests. Each class and many occupations had distinctive uniforms, some of which were prescribed by law. The style of a man's kimono could indicate his rank, the style of a woman's her marital status and age.

With the abolition of the feudal system, these visible signs became less frequently displayed, and some, such as sword carrying by the samurai class, disappeared altogether. As Japan modernized, large commercial conglomerates, such as Mitsui, Mitsubishi, and Sumitomo, that later were called *zaibatsu* (zye-baht-sue), began to replace clans as the primary group affiliation of many.

This new system resulted in the appearance of many new ranks covering a broader spectrum of people, and making it impossible for individuals to identify others by visible signs—although company lapel buttons came to replace the old feudal clan crests. While identifying each other was no longer a life-or-deathissue, it remained of vital importance because it related directly to one's social and business success.

It was essential for businessmen and professionals to be able to quickly establish their company or group affiliation and ranking. Otherwise, etiquette restraints would make it virtually impossible for them to communicate properly.

The name card came to serve this vital function. The regular use of name cards was apparently begun centuries ago in China by an imperial court eunuch who rose to the position of minister of the empire. He favored very large, pink cards. Name cards did not become common in Japan, however, until after 1868, the year marking the fall of the last shogunate and the abolition of the samurai and clan systems.

Despite the changes in the national government and the abolition of the feudalistic clans, more than two thousand years of cultural conditioning could not be swept away overnight or even in several generations. Class, rank, and seniority consciousness remained the paramount forces controlling interpersonal relationships in Japanese society. This fundamental factor was to propel name cards into a vital role in Japanese life.

The manner of exchanging name cards, called *meishi kōkan* (may-she koe-kahn), is, of course, ritualized in keeping with the Japanese penchant for carefully structured behavior. And, as may be expected, it requires a substantial amount of know-how and experience to properly exchange name cards in the Japanese way. Three or four inexperienced visitors trying to exchange cards, shake hands, and bow to a group of Japanese businessmen can present quite a comedy.

The first point uninitiated visitors should keep in mind is that exchanging name cards should be done slowly and methodically. You should face the individual you are giving your card to, hold your card with both hands with the printing facing the recipient, and, as you receive the other person's card, say your name along with one of the usual greetings such as: *Tanaka desu. Hajimemashite, dōzo yoroshiku.* (tah-nah-ka dess. hah-jee-may-mahsh-tay, doe-zoe yoe-roshe-kuu.) This is the equivalent of "My name is Tanaka. I'm pleased to meet you."

As soon as you receive the other person's card you should look at his name and title, determine the degree of respect due him, and then bow accordingly. Remember to turn slightly to the side to avoid bumping heads if you are close together.

If the person you have just met is significantly senior to you and you want to make a strong, positive impression on him for whatever reason, your bow should be fairly deep (forty-five degrees) and should be held for two or three seconds. (For more information on bowing, see Chapter 9.)

If you are senior and there is no reason for you to cater to the individual, your bow can be shallower and shorter. The procedure is the same for each individual in a group. Keep in mind that the exchange should not be hurried. Also remember, if you are introducing yourself to several people, that it is impolite to deal your cards as if you were playing poker.

Of course, there will be occasions when you are across a table or in some other awkward situation where you cannot follow the correct procedure. On such occasions, apologizing for not being able to do it correctly is in order. You will be covered if you say something like *shitsurei shimasu* (she-tsoo-ray she-mahss), which means more or less "pardon me" or "I am being rude."

If you have your name, title, and company printed in Japanese as well as in English on your card, make sure that the Japanese side is right side up and faces the person receiving the card when you hand it to someone. Having your card printed in both Japanese and English is important if you are doing business with Japanese companies. One reason this is important is that Japanese cannot pronounce many foreign names just from their English spelling. It is better if the names are transcribed into Japanese syllables; for example Mr. Greenberg to *Misuta Guriinbāgu* (meese-tah guu-reen-baah-guu), and Smith to *Sumisu* (sue-mee-sue).

It is also good etiquette to keep your name cards in some kind of plastic or leather holder. This not only keeps them together but also helps prevent them from becoming smudged and worn. It is impolite to hand out a less-than-pristine card.

9

Bowing

From the earliest times, bowing has been the Japanese method of expressing greetings, saying farewell, paying respect, apologizing, showing humility, and indicating understanding and acceptance. The custom, which is common to many societies, no doubt had its origins in the animalistic behavior of demonstrating submissiveness by dropping to the ground or lowering the head to avoid conflict with a stronger adversary. In particular, it likely became an institutionalized form of etiquette in religiously oriented societies where such behavior was considered proper when in the presence of deities and their earthly representatives.

As with so many other behavioral traits, the Japanese took the practice of bowing much further than most people, developing it to a fine art and making it the only acceptable act in many different social situations. During feudal times, failing to bow at the expected time or bowing improperly to a samurai or lord could result in a death sentence, sometimes carried out on the spot.

In earlier years, training in bowing began before babies could walk. In fact, their mothers and others would push their heads and trunks down repeatedly on the numerous daily occasions when bowing was the proper protocol. By the time children had reached school age, bowing was automatic, almost instinctive. The educational system and the maturing process honed bowing know-how, making it an integral part of the Japanese personality and character.

There are three specific types of bow: the light bow, the medium bow, and the deep bow. The latter, called *sai-keirei* (sigh-kay-ray), or "highest form of salutation," was commonly used during the shogunate period (1192–1868), but following the downfall of the last shogun in 1868, it was for the most part used only toward the emperor.

With the democratization of Japan following the end of World War II, the emperor renounced his divinity, and the use of the *sai-keirei* to pay obeisance to him gradually declined. Except for traditionalists—who are usually elderly—he is now treated like any other dignitary, i.e., when greeting him a medium bow has come to be entirely proper.

With the medium or formal bow the arms are extended downward with the hands resting on the legs above the knees. The body is then bent to about a forty-five-degree angle. The longer the bow is held the more meaning it has. In a normal situation it is held for only two or three seconds.

With the light bow, the one most often used today, the body is bent to about a twenty-degree angle and the bow is held for only a second or so. The hands should be down at the sides when executing the light bow, but there are numerous occasions when this is impractical, such as when you are carrying something. The position of the hands has thus become more or less incidental, although it is polite to make an effort to bring them down to your sides.

Generally speaking, the medium bow is used when greeting dignitaries, when meeting those who are significantly senior to you and to whom you want to show a special degree of respect, and when expressing especially strong feelings of humility, sorrow, or apology to anyone.

If you are in a situation where you encounter the same dignitaries or highly placed seniors several times in one day, you should greet them with a medium bow the first time you meet them that day and a light bow thereafter.

The influence of the bow in Japanese society is so powerful that foreign residents who are studying the language and associate frequently with Japanese are susceptible to picking up the custom by osmosis. I still sometimes catch myself bowing when I am talking to a Japanese on the telephone!

Young, urban Japanese mothers virtually gave up the custom of teaching their children from infancy the custom of bowing. Nowadays, children are required to bow in school and on numerous other social occasions, but the practice is not being instilled into their reflexes or psyche, as it had been in the past. Young people entering the work force from the 1980s, especially those entering the retail service industry, have had to be taught to bow as part of their company training.

The bow remains a vital part of daily life and work in Japan, and it is not likely to disappear within the foreseeable future even though the younger generations are assuming a much more casual attitude toward it. There is, in fact, a pronounced tendency among Japanese to gradually revert to traditional attitudes and forms of behavior as they age. They find many of the old customs more satisfying and fulfilling than practices copied from the West.

The foreign visitor does not have to be overly concerned about when and how to bow when dealing with Japanese. Once again, Japanese regard the bow as a custom of their own particular culture and tend to believe that foreigners cannot be expected to do it properly— although to not make any attempt at all may still be regarded as impolite or arrogant.

The best rule to follow in a one-on-one situation is to bow when the Japanese do and to be wary of bowing too low or for too long when the occasion does not call for it. In other words, it is better to err on the conservative side to avoid being considered insincere or foolish.

Customers at department stores and other public places are not expected to return the repeated bows of store employees. But the bow of a receptionist in a company lobby should be acknowledged with a slight nodding of the head. A casual nod of the head is also all that is usually called for in hotels and in restaurants, places where the staff regularly bows to guests.

Keep in mind that deep, long bows are reserved for occasions when one demonstrates extraordinary appreciation, respect, humility, or sorrow. Again, older people, especially longtime friends who do not see each other often, will typically bow deep and long as a way of expressing deeply felt emotions. When such bows involve old friends, they are the Japanese equivalent of a warm embrace.

10

Shaking Hands Japanese-Style

Personal relationships in Japan have been complicated a bit by the introduction of the Western handshake. As with other areas of Japanese culture, the new import has not replaced the traditional act—the bow—or reduced its importance. Most Japanese now use a fairly smooth combination of bow and handshake.

Problems arise for foreign visitors when there is a question about whether to mix the two, or which comes first, especially when name cards are being exchanged. Most Western visitors will automatically put their hands out as soon as any introduction begins and before there is time to exchange name cards or bow, and this can make the meeting awkward.

Interestingly, many Japanese will both bow and shake hands when they are meeting for the first time, but generally they will exchange name cards first, bow, and then shake hands. Those who are experienced at meeting foreign visitors, however, usually proceed without any false starts, shaking hands first and then exchanging name cards and bows.

Visitors should keep the customary Japanese order in mind when being introduced. Exchange name cards first, bow while repeating your name, then shake hands. Of course, if the Japanese party offers his hand immediately, it is perfectly all right to take it. But the point is to have the presence of mind to do it the Japanese way either by taking the lead or by instantly following their lead when they begin reaching for their name cards (instead of extending their hands).

The above situation can become a mess when five or six visitors are introduced to a number of Japanese and there is a cross-cultural mix-up. Courtesy requires that visitors in Japan should attempt to follow Japanese customs in such situations. To do so requires both awareness of the cultural differences and the presence of mind necessary to adjust one's behavior to fit the occasion.

11

Seating

Japanese society was tradi-
tionally arranged vertically, with superiors placed over
inferiors in a hierarchy of ranks that extended from the
emperor above to the lowest commoner below. Grada-
tions were minutely defined and separations were
meticulously maintained. The physical positioning of
people demonstrated as well as maintained class, rank,
age, and sex divisions.

In any situation involving two or more people, the
senior or ranking individual took, or was given, the place
of honor. Of course, this is a custom in virtually all
societies, but, as usual, in Japan it was carried to the
extreme.

The last legal sanctions involving divisions by class,
rank, or other criteria were abolished in 1945 (during
the first months of the American military occupation),
but some of the customs were so deeply rooted that they
continued. One such custom is seating or standing order,
which adult Japanese will automatically establish according to accepted rules of etiquette.

In any semiformal situation, from a photo session to
a casual meeting in a coffee shop, restaurant, or company conference room, a Japanese group will sort itself

out according to real or perceived rank and give the *kami-za* (kah-me-zah), or "seat of honor," to the ranking person or guest.

When there is a foreign visitor in the group, one of the Japanese will invariably assume a leadership role and direct him to the seat regarded as appropriate for his rank and the occasion. If he is a respected, valued guest, he will normally be seated in or next to the place of honor.

In any room, the place of honor is usually the seat (or desk or table) farthest from the entrance and located at what might be called the "head" of the room. In a room with a window or windows on only one side, that side is generally designated as the head of the room.

There is also a position of honor in an elevator (in the center nearest the back wall), in a car (the backseat behind the driver), at a head table (in the center of the table away from and opposite the door), in a train coach (the window seat or the center seat), in the first-class cabin of an airplane (a window seat about midcabin, on the right side away from the door), when walking with a group (the center of the group), etc.

When your hosts are Japanese, it is proper to let them designate where you should sit. It is very improper to take the initiative and seat yourself in the place of honor, as ignorant visitors sometimes inadvertently do. If you are the host, it is very important that you direct the ranking Japanese guest to the seat or place of honor and *not* accept a no or any show of reluctance on his part, even if you have to use some degree of playful force.

In public places such as theaters or open seating on trains you can "save" a seat by leaving an article of clothing or some other possession on it.

12

Dining Etiquette

Perhaps no other area of the lives of ordinary Japanese has been more carefully prescribed or ritualized than the simple process of eating. As a result of the overall cultural emphasis on defining, classifying, categorizing, and systemizing, the early Japanese turned the preparation, presentation, and consumption of food into, firstly, a ritualized aesthetic experience and, secondly, a culinary experience.

Meals at the imperial court, at the court of the shogun, in the castles of the provincial lords, in the homes of ranking samurai, in Buddhist temples, at traditional inns, and in the homes of well-to-do merchants were exquisite exercises in stylized service and beautiful blends of colors, textures, and tastes as carefully choreographed as a Kabuki play.

The beauty of the food, the artistic complement of the tableware, the formal manner of the service, and the proper dining etiquette were considered among the highest levels of cultural expression, indicative of one's character and refinement.

The centuries-long devotion of Japan's middle and upper classes to such high-level dining naturally influenced the lower classes, but it was more the huge number of inns that sprang up in the 1600s that brought the custom of ritualized dining to the masses.

In the late 1630s, the third Tokugawa shogun decreed that nearly all of the country's 270 or so provincial lords must keep their families in the shogun's capital of Edo (present-day Tokyo) at all times, and that the lords, along with large retinues, would spend every other year in Edo in attendance at the court of the shogun.

This required that huge numbers of people travel to and from Edo, on foot, throughout the year, as the clan lords with their samurai guards, servants, and retainers made the annual trek. Immediately after this edict went into effect, inns to accommodate the masses of travelers began springing up every few miles along the main roads to Edo.

At every official way station along the nation's great thoroughfares, there were three classes of inns: luxury inns for the lords and their personal attendants; first-class inns for their ranking retainers; and ordinary inns for foot soldiers and lower-ranking retainers.

Also during the early years of the Tokugawa period, religious associations called *kō* (koe) began a system of collecting money from members and then drawing lots to see who went on pilgrimages to famous shrines and temples. This system added greatly to the number of travelers using the new network of inns.

Japan's official "alternate attendance" system continued for some 250 years, and the imperial court style and standard of dining became commonplace. By the beginning of the modern era in 1868, court-style dining strongly influenced the more than one hundred thousand inns throughout the country, and for the most part, the homes of the masses as well.

Present-day inns and traditional restaurants serve in the same age-old manner. Often they offer exactly those foods that were enjoyed by the emperors, shoguns, clan lords, and ranking people of the past.

Dining Japanese-style at a restaurant in one of the beautiful inns that still dot the country remains one of the special joys of visiting Japan. Though eating Japanese-style remains highly ritualized, the visitor can get by with a minimum of skill in using *o-hashi* (oh-hah-she), or chopsticks, and the basics of eating etiquette—and an ability to sit on the floor for an extended period.

If it is your first time with *o-hashi,* the best idea is to ask for a few instructions on how to hold them. If you still have difficulty using them as tongs to grasp pieces of food, just hold the ends close together and use them as a scoop.

Another helpful technique, commonly employed by Japanese, is to pick up your rice bowl and use it more or less as a tray or "safety net" when conveying food to your mouth. Many Japanese meals are served in bowls that can be—and often are—picked up and held close to the chin while eating.

It is also common for people to hold their free hand under the tidbit of food being conveyed to the mouth with *o-hashi*. This is especially useful when you are eating something relatively large and heavy, such as sushi. For that matter, sushi is often eaten with the fingers. In restaurants you are often provided with an *o-shibori* (oh-she-boe-ree), a small dampened cloth, to wipe your hands before eating.

Chopstick taboos include sticking them into your rice and leaving them standing up, and using them to serve yourself from a common dish. If serving chopsticks or some other utensils are not available, reverse your own chopsticks and use the top ends when serving yourself or someone else.

When not in use, chopsticks customarily are placed on small ceramic or bamboo rests. If rests are not provided, lean your chopsticks on the side of a dish or saucer. When you have finished eating, lay the chopsticks across the top of your main dish, plate, or bowl, or across your rice bowl. In formal situations it is proper to lay your chopsticks down when you are being served.

Japanese-style soup is served in small lacquered bowls. You simply pick up the bowl and sip from it as if it were a cup. The ingredients in many such soups settle to the bottom in a matter of seconds and you may stir the soup with your chopsticks before drinking.

Many Japanese diners eat more than one bowl of rice

with their meals. If you finish the first bowl early it is normally assumed that you want a refill. There is no breach of etiquette, however, in eating just one bowl of rice.

When eating the so-called *kaiseki* (kye-say-kee) type meal (a light meal made up of a variety of tiny dishes that originated in Buddhist temples), rice is normally the last main course served. If you simply must have rice to go with the exotic-looking and exotic-tasting tidbits, apologize and order it.

In Japanese-style restaurants where diners eat sitting on tatami floors, it is permissible to ask for a *za-isu* (zah-ee-sue), a legless chair that sits on the floor. This is especially helpful when the meal is a banquet lasting for an hour or more.

13

The Japanese Way of Drinking

As in most ancient agricultural societies, the Japanese discovered how to turn grain into an alcoholic drink very early in their history. A winelike beverage made from rice and called saké was used sacramentally in Shinto ceremonies long before recorded history began.

The use of saké as a tonic for older people gradually

spread among the population. From this stage it was a short step for adults in general to drink saké as a recreational beverage as well as for medicinal purposes.

With full religious sanction, drinking saké eventually became an important component of Japanese society. It was used as a tonic, for recreational purposes, to commemorate special events such as contracts and weddings, to accompany meals, and so on. All public restaurants and inns served saké as a matter of course.

The Japanese quickly took to beer and whiskey when these drinks were introduced from the West in the mid-1800s, and both soon became major industries. The drinking of alcoholic beverages in Japan today is as institutionalized as drinking tea. Saké, however, is still considered the national beverage.

Given the importance of saké and drinking throughout Japanese history, it is not surprising to find that there are numerous points of etiquette applying to drinking. Like so many facets of Japanese etiquette, the rules of drinking are far less strictly adhered to these days, but enough remain in force to make ignoring them seem impolite.

Probably the most conspicuous drinking custom in Japan is for people, especially hosts, to make a special point of pouring the drinks for other people in the party, particularly guests. In cabarets and geisha inns, it is the job of the hostesses and geisha to keep the glasses of the guests topped off. This, in turn, encourages drinking, because it is customary to take at least a sip from the glass or cup each and every time it is refilled. If you decline the offer, however, the worst that will happen is that your reputation as a great party animal will go down a notch or two.

Traditional Japanese drinking etiquette called for the patron or guest to hold his glass or saké cup with both hands when it was being refilled, and to also use both hands when he was pouring for someone else. This custom is not always followed now, but when it is, it instantly marks that person as having exceptionally good manners and probably good character as well.

If you are a guest, and the host or some other member of the party pours a drink for you, you should do the same for them—if they will let you. Some will strongly resist any such effort, either because they want to emphasize that you are the guest, or because they want you to be obligated to them.

Given the Japanese propensity to drink and to expect others to drink, it is often necessary for light drinkers or nondrinkers to draw a line. About the only acceptable reason for not drinking is a medical excuse. Having some kind of weakness that is aggravated by copious drinking can also be used fairly effectively to avoid overdrinking. In my case, it is excessively long-lasting hangovers. In Japanese "hangover" is *futsuka-yoi* (futes-kah-yoe-e), which can be loosely translated as "two-day drunk." I make a joke by saying I suffer from *mikka-yoi* (meek-kah-yoe-e), or "three-day drunk."

However, the most common way to limit one's

drinking is to pretend that you are drunker than you really are. Japanese habitually feign complete drunkenness not only to avoid overdrinking but also to give them an excuse to "break etiquette" and do things they wouldn't ordinarily do, such as behave in a ribald, licentious manner toward hostesses and geisha, when they are actually sober enough to know what they are doing—and to enjoy it.

About the only Japanese men who do not drink, or who drink very lightly, are a surprisingly large number whose metabolism cannot handle alcohol. One or two swallows is usually enough to make them turn beet-red and perspire profusely. If they continue to drink they almost always vomit before the evening is over because their systems reject the alcohol.

Some Japanese hosts are exceptionally forceful in encouraging guests to drink, and it is often necessary to be strong-willed to resist them. Refusing to drink or drinking only moderately must be done with diplomacy —preferably with one of the medical excuses suggested above—because the Japanese believe that the only way you can really get to know a person is to see him drunk.

The reason for this attitude is that the etiquette the Japanese must follow while sober is so strict that their real personalities and characters remain hidden. They are inclined to believe that anyone who refuses to get drunk is either hiding something or is arrogant.

In summary, the best way out of this subtle cultural bind is to drink a little bit and then to let it all hang out. The traditional Japanese drinking toast is *Kanpai!* (kahm-pie), a word all visitors find very useful.

14

Paying the Bill

Japanese are noted for their skill as hosts and for their hospitality. Steeped in protocol, their banquets and parties are often too stereotyped and too rigidly controlled for Western tastes, but once you get beyond the cultural barriers, outings with Japanese friends can be a wonderful experience.

Of course, being able to speak Japanese and participate in the jokes and conversation makes any party much better, but parties can be fun for anyone who is not shy about enjoying himself.

There is one point of Japanese party protocol, however, that often presents foreign visitors with a dilemma. This is the habit the Japanese have of insisting on paying for restaurant or bar bills when that obligation rightfully belongs to the foreigner. I have seen and been personally involved in actual physical struggles to obtain possession of a check.

This behavior has been a national characteristic for centuries, and certainly does not derive from the economic success of the country. I think it is an expression of pride, mixed with a strong desire to demonstrate equality if not superiority. These feelings were nurtured during the long Tokugawa shogunate, Japan's last feudal dynasty, when classes were established by law. Profit-making through commerce was considered the lowest of all callings and the display of affluence was prohibited. In these circumstances, one of the few ways members of the merchant class could demonstrate their business acumen and financial superiority was in profligate spending on entertainment. Tokugawa history abounds with stories of ordinary people going to extremes to extend extraordinary hospitality and to outspend others in situations where such displays were strictly for show and the personal satisfaction involved. A touch of this apparently remains in the Japanese character.

Some visitors confronted with the cost of having fun in Japan are only too happy to have someone else pick up the tab. That is fine if you are clearly a guest. But if you are just as clearly the host, or it is obviously your turn to pay, allowing someone else to pay the bill is both unfair and demeaning.

When you *should* pay the bill—or want to pay it—it is best to pay in advance or to leave the party before it ends, pay the bill, and then return. This latter approach is not only the easiest but is also the correct etiquette, because displaying or talking about money is also considered ill-mannered and beneath the dignity of a cultured person.

15

Public Etiquette

One of the many puzzling contradictions of the Orient is that the Japanese, internationally renowned for their refined, stylized manners and unfailing courtesy, are also infamous for being rude in public, uncaring about strangers, and heedless of the environment. While Japanese public rudeness and callous attitude toward strangers, which has been exaggerated to some extent, has significantly lessened in recent decades, the concepts of public awareness and concern for outsiders remain relatively undeveloped.

Once again, historical factors explain why the Japanese tend to reject any responsibility for the environment or for strangers. For centuries the focus of responsibility in Japan was extremely narrow and limited to the family, the work group, the village, and the local authority. Each unit of this vertical grouping was exclusive and in competition with every other unit.

Japan's clan system, which pitted the clans against each other and endured until 1868, contributed to the group-against-group mentality, as each clan strove to be totally self-sufficient and to improve its ranking with respect to other clans (goals clearly discernible in Japanese companies today).

The Japanese thus became group oriented to the point that there was little or no communication or cooperation with other groups. The only way you could become a member of one of these groups was to be born into it or to enter it at the very bottom when young. Outsiders were either ignored or considered potential enemies.

Although Japan has converted from a feudal agricultural society to a high-tech urban society, the social scenario is still one of thousands of groups competing against each other. To make one's group better than every other group is still the primary motivating force and often the only responsibility that is taken seriously. On a national level this obsession to be the first, the biggest, or the best makes Japan a formidable international competitor.

As Japanese sociologists and management gurus point out, the Japanese work exceptionally well within their own groups, but have little or no affinity for working with other groups or taking individual responsibility for things outside of their immediate work area. Translated into public behavior, this means most Japanese are inclined to ignore everything and everybody not somehow related to them or their group.

Travelers in Japan may confront the public-etiquette face of the Japanese in many situations. Such incidents can be quite irritating—though rarely serious. It is common for intoxicated men on late-night commuter trains, for example, to sprawl all over seats and other passengers, and to throw up. Oddly enough, Japanese drunks are often attracted to foreign faces in the crowd and will sometimes approach visitors to either strike up a conversation or to insult them. One way to avoid involvement with drunks is to never look them in the eye. If you do, it may be interpreted as an invitation to talk or a challenge to fight. The best thing to do if you encounter a drunk is to quickly and quietly move away.

Public displays of affection, once taboo in Japan, are now commonplace among the young. They usually involve no more than intertwining arms or holding hands while walking, still relatively tame by Western standards. The action in parks frequented by the young is often more intense, however.

During the Tokugawa shogunate the clothing of the different social classes in Japan was prescribed by the government. The dress code went so far as to designate the dates on which people changed from winter to summer clothing and vice versa. As a result, the Japanese became especially sensitive to the relationship of clothing to class and privilege.

When Western-style clothing was introduced into Japan, the Japanese tended to dress much more conservatively than their Western counterparts. The first ones to break with the conservative traditions of the past were the teenage girls who became involved with the Occupation forces following the war. As early as the late 1940s they began braving the anger of their parents by dressing in bright-colored clothing, wearing high heels, and applying lipstick.

Japanese youth today are very casual, individualistic, and often flamboyant in their informal clothing. Older people still tend to be more conservative—and more fashionable—than their foreign counterparts. Good designer brand names, particularly in sports and casual wear, are the standard. Visitors to Japan who conform to dress codes acceptable in Western capitals, in both formal and informal situations, will fit right in.

A traditional taboo in Japan was the practice of eating while walking in public. An exception to the rule was at festivals, where snacks were sold from stalls. Patrons of street vendors generally ate before leaving the area or took their purchases home with them.

The taboo against eating in public began breaking down with the appearance of fast-food outlets that had little or no inside seating and offered take-out service. The first McDonald's in Japan, which opened in the front of the Matsuya department store in Ginza on July 20, 1971, had no seating at all. Most customers ate while standing or milling around on the sidewalk in front of the shop. Some of the new ice cream shops also had only service counters fronting on the sidewalk.

Pedestrians eating in public are still rare enough today to be conspicuous and regarded as ill-mannered. Visitors concerned with conveying a good image while in Japan should limit their eating in public to accepted occasions and areas—including picnics, flower-viewing parties, hiking, long-distance train rides and sightseeing buses, as well as the immediate vicinity of fast-food counters and street vendors.

An act related to Japanese etiquette that foreign visitors may encounter is an older Japanese stopping suddenly to bow when unexpectedly meeting a friend. This may happen while walking along a crowded sidewalk or in a department store aisle. Fast reflexes are necessary to avoid a collision if you are directly behind them.

Changes in child-raising methods in Japan, especially in urban areas, have resulted in a revolution in the behavior of children, both in private and in public. Prior to 1960 it was exceedingly rare to hear or see a Japanese baby cry. Noisy, rowdy behavior by older children in public places was also almost nonexistent. Crying babies and rowdy children are now a common part of the public scene and sometimes cause disturbances in restaurants and stores. Rightly or not, Western influence is often blamed for the breakdown in Japan's traditional child-rearing system.

16

Public Transportation

Mass transportation in Japan is just that—masses of people pressed into buses, subways, and trains, particularly during morning and evening rush hours. At these times, most forms of transportation carry from three to four times their rated capacity.

With such huge numbers of people dependent upon public transportation, the Japanese have taken advantage of their genius for organization and of the latest technologies to develop extraordinarily efficient transportation systems. These systems interconnect bus, subway, and train lines, and facilitate the rapid movement of millions of people every day throughout the entire country.

In the first decade and a half of Japan's postwar democratic period (1945–60), getting on and off trains was a free-for-all that often left people injured. But as transportation systems improved, the traditional Japanese penchant for order reasserted itself, and despite the increasingly larger crowds of commuters, using the system became much safer.

Today, places on boarding platforms where individual coaches stop are clearly marked, and commuters generally line up in an orderly fashion. Visitors should keep in mind, however, that from about 7:30 to 9:30 a.m. and 5:00 to 7:00 p.m. the masses of commuters are such that getting in and out of coaches can be a challenge.

During the heaviest part of the rush hour, platform workers are brought in at some stations to literally push the last passengers onto the cars, packing them in so tight it is virtually impossible for those standing in

the vicinity of the doors to move. In winter heavy clothing results in even more crowding.

Visitors are advised to avoid using public transportation during the worst of the rush hours. If you must
travel during these periods it is best to give yourself a
few minutes leeway, and not board until you are in front
of the line (let other waiting commuters pass you). When
the stream of disembarking passengers stops, board very
quickly and if possible position yourself in one of the
corners just inside the door, turning your back to the
crowd and holding on so you are not pushed into
the middle of the aisle where there is nothing to hold
on to. This maneuver will prevent you from being shoved
further and further into the coach, reducing the possibility of losing your balance as the car starts and stops
and sways from side to side and making it easier to dis-
embark when you come to your stop.

There are doors on both sides of the coaches and the
side that opens varies from station to station. If you do
not know which doors open at your stop, and you guess
wrong (after you have wedged yourself into a door corner), you are usually still better off than if you were
packed into the middle of the aisle, where you get buf-
feted each time there is an exchange of passengers.

Station maps appear on panels above most of the
coach doors, allowing you to identify your stop in advance and begin working your way toward an exit. If
you are caught in the aisle well away from the doors,
it is best to do your maneuvering when the train is

stopped at a station and other people are pushing their way toward the exits.

The extraordinary crowding of Japan's transportation system often results in close, prolonged body contact among standing passengers. Proper etiquette in this situation is to keep your hands still, remain as passive as possible, and avoid direct eye contact. Some people read if there is enough room to hold reading material. Many close their eyes—and some of those sitting fall asleep.

17

Bathing

Most visitors to Japan are curious about bathing etiquette because they have heard stories of public baths and mixed-sex bathing or perhaps seen titillating scenes in such movies as *Shogun*. Actually, engaging in premarital or extramarital sex has never been associated in Japan with sin in the Christian sense. Sex was considered a natural function and nudity in its proper place, such as the bath, was not regarded as licentious, suggestive, sinful, scandalous, or anything else.

When foreign missionaries first arrived in Japan in the 1540s, they were horrified by the Japanese custom of bathing regularly and bathing together. Europeans at that time believed daily bathing was harmful to the health. The fact that Japanese men and women bathed together was even more of a shock.

At first the missionaries tried to totally prohibit their new Japanese converts from bathing. When this didn't work they gave them permission to bathe every two weeks. This also failed, so they finally approved of weekly bathing. Among other results of the ignorance and arrogance of these early missionaries to Japan was that they and their Japanese converts smelled bad.

Missionaries were expelled from Japan in the late 1500s and early 1600s and were not allowed back in until after the fall of the Tokugawa shogunate in the 1860s. In the intervening centuries the missionary orders had learned nothing new about the human condition, and once back in Japan continued their opposition to Japanese-style bathing.

The age-old Japanese custom of daily bathing together in large public baths as well as in private baths survived both missionaries and other social changes until the early 1950s when Japanese female members of the new postwar democratic Diet prevailed upon the government to pass legislation making it mandatory for public baths to segregate the sexes. However, the new mixed-bathing taboo did not apply to private baths in homes, hotels, inns, or spas, where mixed bathing continues today.

Guests at hotels, inns, or hot-spring spas in Japan

usually have a choice of mixed, unmixed, or totally private bathing. Older inns and spas may not, however, have private bathing facilities. Accommodations with Japanese-style bathing usually indicate the available bathing facilities in their brochures. Baths specifically for families are called *kazoku-buro* (kah-zoe-kuu-buu-roe), or "family baths."

The water in spas and other private baths may be very hot. Unless you are in a private bath, however, it is not proper to add cold water to make it more comfortable.

Adventurous visitors to Japan often take advantage of neighborhood public baths, or *sentō* (sen-toe), where people without baths in their homes go for their daily ablutions. Public bathhouses appeared to be on the verge of becoming obsolete by the 1970s, but the proprietors rallied by adding various new services such as adjoining video-game rooms and coin laundries, and were soon back on their feet. The number of *sentō,* however, is definitely on the decline.

Bathing etiquette in Japan is quite simple. Take your own soap and towel, and a washcloth or small hand towel called *tenugui* (tay-nuu-gooey), which is used to cover your genitals when walking around and for scrubbing and sponging off. People going to public baths usually take their own wash pans. Leave your clothing in the dressing room, enter the bathing room, go to a set of wall faucets, and sit down on a wooden or plastic stool. Douse yourself with water and then scrub thoroughly.

After rinsing off, enter the tub or pool of hot water to soak.

In winter some people "cheat" by merely dousing themselves with several buckets of hot water and entering the tub without scrubbing. After they warm up they get out of the tub, scrub, and then get back in for a final soaking. This, of course, dirties the tub water even though it is being continuously replenished with clean water.

If the water is very hot, you may want to rinse off with cool water after leaving the tub. Once out of the tub, sponge off with your *tenugui* and return to the dressing room to finish drying.

In some older baths the only source of hot water is the main tub itself, in which case there will be a bucket or large dipper on hand to take water out of the tub for washing and rinsing.

Many visitors to Japan, particularly men, choose to do some of their bathing in "soaplands" (formerly known as Turkish baths). These are baths with private rooms that feature massages along with various sexual services provided by scantily clad, attractive young women. A few of the soaplands cater exclusively to female clientele.

Some of Japan's male-oriented massage bathhouses are called saunas instead of soaplands (especially in Nagoya). And some of them have steam rooms that will accommodate several people. Most of these saunas offer the same types of services that keep the soaplands thriving.

18

Gift-Giving

The need to maintain harmony in Japan's feudalistic society, in which the rights of the people were not protected by law and the rights of those in power were unrestrained, must have contributed to the Japanese penchant for gift-giving on a gargantuan scale. In feudalistic Japan, gift-giving developed into a highly structured ritual, requiring extensive knowledge to perform properly.

Gifts were given, generally by inferiors to superiors or people in positions of power, to build goodwill, maintain good relations, solicit favors, get out of difficulties, and avoid getting on the bad side of anyone in a position to do harm.

In the early centuries, items that came to be prized as gifts included special foods, silk fabrics, pieces of lacquerware, and other handicraft items. Since the method of presentation was as important as the gifts themselves, a whole packaging industry grew up to serve the gift-giving custom. Packaging became refined to the point that it could be considered a fine art.

With the emergence of a more democratic society in Japan after 1945, gift-giving customs changed. Now, in addition to those occasions where gift-giving is still important in making and nurturing good relations and securing favors, it is also practiced by companies on a massive scale as a gesture of goodwill to customers and as tokens of appreciation for past business. Two great annual gift-giving seasons are now so important in the Japanese economy that they make up a significant percentage of the annual sales of many manufacturers, wholesalers, and retailers. These two seasons are *O-chūgen* (oh-chuu-gen) in midsummer and *O-seibo* (oh-say-boe) in early December.

Giving the right gifts to the right people during these two periods is an important social obligation in Japan. Because the know-how of seasonal gift-giving (and gift etiquette at weddings and funerals) is no longer automatically transmitted from parents to offspring, guidebooks on these subjects are perennial bestsellers.

Originally, midsummer gifts were given during the ancient *O-bon* (oh-bone), or Festival of the Dead, in remembrance of those who had died during the preceding year. Nowadays, midyear gifts might be classified as "good relations" gifts, while those given at the end of the year are regarded as "appreciation" gifts—for favors, business, loyalty, etc.

Beginning in the 1970s, Valentine's Day quickly developed into a major occasion, a phenomenon that some cynics accused the chocolate industry of masterminding. Valentine's Day in Japan, however, comes with a twist—women alone give boxes of chocolates to men.

Birthdays, graduations, vacation travel, and other auspicious events are also established occasions for gift-giving, as are weddings, when all guests give *and* receive gifts. Authorities, celebrities, and individuals interviewed by the news media regularly receive gifts or cash. It is also still common to give gifts to people who provide information, advice, or offer other assistance.

The variety of gifts is now virtually unlimited, but there are certain gifts that are appropriate for specific occasions and not for others. Here are some of the regular gift-giving occasions and their appropriate gifts:

BEREAVEMENT
Money, incense, flowers, fruit, and other food items.

BIRTHDAY
Money, clothing, accessories, candy, sports equipment, tapes, videos, records, etc. The 60th, 70th, 78th, 88th, and 99th birthdays are special occasions in Japan and are marked by special parties and elaborate gifts.

SUMMER GIFT-GIVING SEASON *(O-chūgen)*
Alcoholic drinks, fruit packages, coffee, candy, cooking oils, seaweed (dried sheets of processed seaweed used in various Japanese dishes).

GET-WELL GIFTS
Money, fruit, other foods, flowers (visiting someone who is sick or has been in an accident is an institutionalized

custom called *o-mimai* (oh-me-my). It should be noted that a potted plant is often not a welcome gift. A common superstition has it that the roots of the plant symbolize a long hospital stay—literally being "rooted" in bed.

GRADUATION
Apparel, personal accessories, travel accessories, gift certificates, money.

O-SEIBO YEAR-END GIFT-GIVING SEASON
Beer, wine, whiskey, bulk food items, calendars.

PROMOTION
Personal accessories, wine, whiskey, sports equipment.

SEVEN-FIVE-THREE FESTIVAL *(Shichi-Go-San)*
This festival centers around a ceremonial shrine visit for boys aged five and girls aged three and seven. Money, apparel, toys, and recreational equipment are the usual gifts.

TRAVEL
When Japanese travel, especially abroad, they customarily take a supply of small gifts called *o-tsukai mono* (oh-tsoo-kye moc-no), or "things to be used," to give to people they meet and particularly to those who do them favors. These gifts range from hand towels,

Japanese paper, fans, and scarves to inexpensive calcu-
lators. While traveling, people often buy famous local
products or specialty products to give to family
members, friends, and company colleagues upon their
return. These gifts are called *o-miyage* (oh-mee-yah-gay).

VISITING
Fruit, cake, cookies, seaweed, candy, coffee, and other
food items.

WEDDINGS
Money is the most common gift for weddings. It is
invariably presented in the form of crisp, new ten-
thousand-yen notes in a special money envelope called
a *noshibukuro* (no-she-buu-kuu-roe), sold at stationers.
The minimum (for the wedding of a casual acquaintance) is ten thousand yen.

As mentioned earlier, gift-wrapping is a special art
in Japan. Customarily, gifts are wrapped in two sheets
of white handmade paper and tied with special cords—
mizuhiki (me-zuu-hee-kee)—made of rolled paper. Black-
and-white cords are reserved for bereavement gifts; red,
silver, and gold cords for happy occasions. Weddings and
deaths call for the cords to be tied in square knots,
representing permanence. Bows are acceptable on other
occasions.

Naturally, there is a correct Japanese way to fold
wrapping paper around a package. When the gifts are

for happy events, the right side of the paper goes over the left side. When the gifts are expressions of sadness, the wrapping is reversed.

Foreign visitors and residents in Japan are not expected to follow precisely Japanese protocol in wrapping gifts, but failure to give a gift on a gift-giving occasion may be regarded as insensitivity to Japanese customs.

Gift-wrapping need pose no problem, however, as most stores will provide the proper wrapping at the sales counter upon request. Gifts are wrapped in paper decorated with the store's logo, but unlike in the West, such paper is totally acceptable and even preferable when the store is one that is well known and respected.

The volume of gifts received by Japanese had become so great by the 1980s that many gifts went unused. Companies set up specifically to buy unopened, unwanted gifts (at a fraction of their original cost) appeared on the scene. These companies sell the unused gifts at substantial discounts.

19

Home-Visiting Etiquette

Japanese do not have an established custom of inviting friends to their homes, simply because their homes have traditionally been small, crowded, and considered inappropriate for entertaining. Instead, it became the practice to invite people to public drinking places and restaurants—one of the reasons Japan has more restaurants and drinking places per capita than any other nation.

Prior to modern times it was, in fact, more likely that the Japanese would invite foreign friends to their homes rather than other Japanese. It is still unusual for the average Japanese, particularly older people, to invite longtime friends, much less casual acquaintances, to their homes. However, with growing Westernization, newfound affluence, and the construction of larger homes and apartments that are all or mostly Western-style, such invitations are becoming more common.

Once you are inside the home, etiquette remains essentially the same whether the home is Western-style or Japanese-style, although in a Japanese-style home one sits on *tatami* (tah-tah-me), reed-mat flooring, and food or refreshments are served on a low table.

Should you be invited to a traditional Japanese-style home, you will find that the front sliding door of the house is usually not locked and that there may not be an outside doorbell. The proper etiquette is to open the door and enter (some old homes have bells attached to the doors that will ring when they are opened). You will then be standing in a small, ground-level vestibule called the *genkan* (gen-kahn). Once inside the *genkan* you should call out *Gomen kudasai!* (go-men kuu-dah-sigh), which more or less means "Excuse me!"

If you expect to be invited in, and you are wearing a raincoat or overcoat (or hat and gloves), remove them before the host arrives to welcome you. There will be a place in the *genkan* for umbrellas, and sometimes hooks for raincoats and overcoats. If there are no coat hooks, hand your coat to the host if he or she offers to take it, or carry it with you when you are invited in. If you carry your coat into the guest or living room, the common procedure is to fold it and place it on the floor next to the wall behind you (you normally sit around a table placed in the center of the room).

The floor level of the house will normally be about four to twelve inches above the level of the *genkan*. Remove your street shoes before stepping up onto the main level. Your host will invariably place a pair of slippers on the floor in front of you.

The trick is to get your shoes off without falling down or having to sit down, and to step directly from your shoes onto the main level. (When Japanese houses were designed, the people did not wear lace-up shoes. They wore thonged sandals or wooden clogs.) If you must sit down to get your shoes off, apologize before doing so. It is especially bad form to touch the *genkan* floor with your stocking feet because this tracks dirt into the house. Because of the custom of removing one's shoes before entering a home, slip-on shoes have always been popular. Long-handled shoehorns are also standard equipment in *genkan*.

After you are up on the wooden landing, put on the

slippers and follow your host down the hall. The slippers are not worn into rooms that have reed-mat floors. They are for wood floors only and are left in the hallway. (A semi-Western house may have a Western-style sitting room with a wooden floor or a carpet over it. In this case the host will expect you to keep the slippers on.)

In a typical Japanese-style *tatami* room you will be provided with a *za-buton* (zah-buu-tone), floor cushion, to sit on. Traditional etiquette calls for you to first sit directly on the reed-mat floor and not move onto the floor cushion until your host invites you to do so a second time.

The old Japanese way of sitting, on closed, folded legs, is rapidly disappearing, and you certainly won't be expected to sit that way. You may sit cross-legged, or with your legs and feet pulled up and at your side.

Seating etiquette invariably comes into play when you are invited into a Japanese-style living room. The focal point of the room is the traditional alcove, or *toko-no-ma* (toe-koe-no-mah), in one corner, usually away from the door. The seat of honor is the one nearest the *toko-no-ma*. It is not polite to take this seat without being asked to do so, and it is good manners to decline two or three times when you are directed to it.

Another point of etiquette is that the *toko-no-ma,* which serves as a kind of "altar" of the home, should not be used as a catchall to put things, such as coats, packages, or empty beer bottles.

Once you are seated, your host will soon serve you some kind of drink—tea, coffee, soft drinks, beer, etc., and usually a small snack, such as pastries, fruit, chips, and so on. If the invitation is for lunch or dinner, you can be sure it will be ample. Most Japanese who now host foreign visitors in their homes for meals make a point of finding out in advance what kind of Japanese food their guests prefer.

If you are visiting a very old home in winter, one that does not have modern heating, you may be invited to sit around a *kotatsu* (koe-taht-sue), a quilt-covered table warmed by an electric heater (formerly burning charcoal). In older homes, the floor may be dug out under the table. With your legs extending under the *kotatsu* and the quilt covering you up to your waist, at least the lower half of your body will be kept quite warm.

Sensibly, even Japanese who live in totally Western-style apartments and homes do not wear their street shoes inside. All such homes are designed with a *genkan* area where the shoes are taken off.

Other than the customs of no shoes inside, no slippers on reed-mat floors, no taking the seat of honor without being invited to do so, and no despoiling the *toko-no-ma,* home-visiting etiquette in Japan is basically the same as in the U.S. and European countries. The one exception is the custom of taking a gift—most often pastries, fruit, cookies, or candy, and sometimes whiskey, saké, or wine. This custom is far more strictly adhered to in Japan than in the U.S.

20

Praise

In a society in which adhering strictly to a formalized etiquette is equated with both character and morality, and where lapses have traditionally been harshly dealt with, it is interesting to note that childhood training in etiquette was effected more through praise and example than by threat of punishment.

During infancy and childhood, Japanese are effusively praised when they act appropriately—whether it is bowing correctly, using chopsticks properly, or singing a song well. Once they approach the teen years, however, they are expected to know and abide by proper etiquette, and such compliments become rare—the idea being that performing the proper act in the correct manner and at the appropriate time is simply expected, and does not warrant special praise.

The group orientation of Japanese society also precludes the singling out of individuals for special recognition. When foreign visitors, unaware of this code, compliment individual Japanese, it often embarrasses those receiving the praise and could even make their colleagues envious to the point of never again accepting them as full, trusted members of the group.

Company managers have to be very diplomatic in the way they treat superior employees. The outstanding athlete on a sports team, for example, has to demonstrate an almost ridiculous degree of modesty regarding his skill and accomplishments in order to prevent his teammates from ostracizing him and the public from regarding him as arrogant. The young scientist who makes a breakthrough and is fussed over by the media or other outsiders is put into a difficult position vis-à-vis his superiors and the senior scientist in his group. He must display the greatest humility to keep the inferior-superior relationship in balance.

Direct personal compliments to Japanese professionals by foreigners can have the reverse effect of what is intended. Japanese go to great lengths to identify their goals and devise sensible strategies for achieving them. When such goals are attained, the group as a whole is to be accorded credit. One of the most common gaffes where foreign men are concerned is overeffusive compliments paid to young Japanese women on their appearance, or dress, and offered in the presence of others. Although this may be appropriate when done in private, in a public setting it can be very embarrassing and upset the delicate balance of the woman's relationships with others, especially Japanese men.

Even to Japanese men, compliments made in public are best expressed indirectly, using general terms. It is better to say something like, "I wish I had your talent," than to say "you are so talented."

21

Criticism

Japanese are naturally much more sensitive to criticism than they are to compliments. The origin of their extraordinary sensitivity to criticism surely derives from the importance of correct behavior in their traditional system, since an essential part of proper behavior was to avoid being shamed and shaming others as a result of behaving in an unacceptable manner.

One of the best-known anecdotes dating from Japan's mythological age involves a god who shamed his fellow gods and goddesses by his failure to follow prescribed manners. He was banned from the heavens.

Being shamed by a personal failure or by an implied failure has traditionally been the worst fate that could befall a Japanese. There was an equally powerful feeling that the only way the shame could be expiated was through revenge. If circumstances were such that revenge was impossible—and the matter was important—suicide was the only acceptable alternative.

Suicide among Japan's samurai class was such an accepted method of expiating the sin of violating etiquette during the Tokugawa period (1603–1868) that numerous edicts by the government prohibiting such behavior were ignored. Japanese history, as well as contemporary literature and movies, is filled with acts of revenge or suicide, brought on by someone having been shamed, either because of his own behavior or through the criticism of others.

Even in modern Japan, hardly a year goes by that several ranking executives, shamed by some failure or criticism, do not take their own lives. Young people, criticized by parents or teachers, are also, tragically, prone to commit suicide.

While criticism by foreigners is not likely to bring on a suicide, visitors should nevertheless be careful about criticizing anyone to their face, whether they be immigration or customs officials, hotel clerks, taxi drivers, or whoever. Even when the criticism is fully and obviously deserved, the shame it produces may have unpleasant repercussions. If you have something to get off your chest, report it to the boss or employing organization of the person you wish to criticize.

Foreign residents of Japan, particularly businessmen who work with Japanese on a daily basis, should be extremely cautious when handling situations where criticism of Japanese is warranted. One of the best ways is to use a third party, preferably someone who is older or higher-ranking than the person being criticized and has had considerable experience handling such sensitive matters.

Another approach, without a third party, is to begin the session with praise and compliments and then bring up the bad news indirectly, stressing the positive results you want to achieve without specifically criticizing the person with whom you are speaking. Being especially sensitive to such things, the Japanese "target" will clearly understand that he or she is being criticized, but he will not be put in the position of losing face.

Interestingly, Japanese managers typically criticize staff members openly, in front of their co-workers. The reason for this is that the staff in each section functions as a team, with little difference in duties and obligations and, consequently, treatment by superiors. Disciplining a member openly reinforces the idea that the whole group is responsible for the behavior of its members. This approach is not advisable for foreign managers in Japan, since such an action would likely be taken in a totally different light.

A favorite technique regularly used by Japanese managers is to invite the persons targeted for criticism out drinking after work. After both have drunk enough to forgo normal dictates of etiquette, the manager can frankly say what has been on his mind all along, but, again, in such a way as to help the other party avoid losing face.

Many managers who use the after-hours drinking technique specialize in using humor to remove some of the sting while making their point. It is not necessary for them to be too explicit. Japanese are so attuned to the tenor of such situations that their "cultural telepathy" allows them to get the message loud and clear.

Another point that should be mentioned is that many foreigners, particularly Americans, are chronic complainers about their own country's perceived failings and constantly make critical comments to the Japanese. Rather than endearing the complainers to the Japanese, this kind of behavior is regarded as a cheap attempt to flatter them and drastically lowers the foreigner's image.

22

The Tea Ceremony

Foreigners who are invited to attend a tea ceremony performed by a skilled tea master are fortunate indeed. The tea ceremony, or *cha-no-yu* (chah-no-you), combines Japan's ancient system of aesthetics and etiquette in one setting, one ceremony that attempts to say it all.

The tea ceremony is therefore many elements in one. It is a display of aestheticism and order, an exercise in control of the mind and body, an attempt to attain the ideal interpersonal relationship and harmony with the cosmos, and, in sum, an opportunity to enjoy a very sensual, highly refined style of living.

Japan's Emperor Shomu, who reigned from 724 to 749, is credited with introducing tea drinking into the country after he had been presented some bricks of pressed tea leaves by a famous Chinese priest named Ganjin. Soon after being introduced to the delightful custom, the emperor made a practice of inviting people in for tea. He once invited one hundred Buddhist monks to his palace for a tea party.

During the Heian period (794–1185), a tea made of steamed and dried tea leaves ground into a powder became popular. Called *matcha* (mah-chah), this is the tea still used today in the tea ceremony. But it was not until the fifteenth century that the tea ceremony, under the patronage of Shogun Yoshimasa Ashikaga (1436–90), became a full-fledged aesthetic, philosophical, and spiritual ritual.

Japanese authorities credit Juko Murata, tea master to Shogun Yoshimasa Ashikaga, with adding the artistic and spiritual dimension that was incorporated into *sadō* (sah-doe), or "the way of tea," in the late 1400s. He is also credited with originating the practice of holding the tea ceremony in a special house or room.

Murata introduced the concepts of *wabi* (wah-bee), *sabi* (sah-bee), and *yūgen* (yuu-gen) into the tea ceremony. *Wabi* refers to a richness, fullness, and serenity found in simplicity. *Sabi* refers to solitude, quiet grandeur, age, and naturalness. *Yūgen* is the mysterious, tranquil beauty that exists just below the surface of a thing. Murata's philosophy of *cha-no-yu* was heavily tinged with pathos and the transience of all things.

About a century later, Sen no Rikyu, an Osaka

merchant turned tea master, put even more emphasis on the Zen Buddhist concepts of simplicity, spiritual tranquillity, and communion with nature in his tea ceremonies, reportedly as a way of countering the snobbery and pretension that existed among his fellow merchants at that time. He also introduced the idea of using a simple but carefully designed and furnished rustic tea "hut" that measured only about twelve by thirteen feet and was separate from the pavilion or room where the guests gathered and waited for the ceremony to begin.

Rikyu further formalized the tea ceremony by establishing rules applying to the attitude and responsibility of the tea host. Some of these were: Make sure your guests feel warm in winter and cool in summer; arrange the flowers so they look like wildflowers; make sure the charcoal is properly prepared so the hot water will be just right for the tea; be quick and efficient; be prepared for rain even on a clear day; be attentive toward all of the guests; serve the tea with insight into the souls of your guests.

After attracting the attention of the powerful warlord Hideyoshi Toyotomi, who had become shogun, Rikyu was designated as his tea master. Some time later the warlord demanded Rikyu's daughter as a concubine. The tea master refused. In 1591 the despot ordered the master to commit suicide, which he did after a farewell tea ceremony.

The *suki-ya* (sooki-yah), or teahouse, that came into use after Juko Murata and Sen no Rikyu accommodated a maximum of five persons. It also had a service room where the utensils were washed and readied. The room had two entrances—one for the host and the other for guests. The doorway for guests was very low, requiring that they enter the room on their hands and knees to humble themselves in preparation for the ceremony—another of Rikyu's ideas.

Present-day teahouses vary in size and degree of luxury but the basic design has remained the same. Several tea ceremony schools have emerged, each with its own style. Some are very formal; others are informal and include a full meal made up of a number of small dishes that originated in Buddhist temples. Some groups hold their ceremonies outside. The three leading schools are Ura-senke, Omote-senke, and Mushakoji.

While a tea ceremony can be held at any time on any occasion, there are several traditional times with different forms. *Akatsuki no cha-no-yu* (ah-kaht-ski no chah-no-you), or "sunrise tea ceremony," begins around 3:00 a.m., when the moon is still bright in the sky, and ends by 6:00 a.m. *Asa no cha-no-yu* (ah-sah no chah-no-you), or "morning tea ceremony," begins around 6:00 a.m. and is popular in the summer months when it is still cool early in the morning. *Shōgo no saji* (show-go no sah-jee), or "noon tea," begins at noon and lasts for three or more hours. *Yoban'ashi no cha-no-yu* (yoe-bahn-ah-she no chah-no-you), or "leisurely evening tea ceremony," usually begins around 6:00 p.m. and lasts as long as the guests want to stay. Finally, there is the *rinji cha-no-yu* (reen-jee chah-no-you), or "special tea ceremony," which is usually held on short notice to mark the visit of a special friend or guest or to celebrate an especially beautiful time of the year, such as when the cherry trees are blooming or when there has been a heavy snowfall.

It should be noted that some kind of light food is served at virtually all tea ceremonies to prepare the stomach for the tea, which is very strong (and possibly unpalatable to those not accustomed to it).

Several tea-ceremony schools and organizations offer ceremonies that are designed to attract large numbers of people. These ceremonies tend to be very commercialized, with the operation of a profitable business being the primary aim. Very little of the deeper meaning of the traditional ceremony comes through at these sessions.

A traditional tea ceremony begins when a host invites guests and begins preparing for the ceremony, usually a number of days in advance. The site for the ceremony should always be a quiet place where interruptions are unlikely. On the day of the ceremony, the host carefully sweeps and waters down the outside area, then cleans the tearoom and utensils and prepares any special dishes to be served.

The host generally greets the guests in the waiting room and then withdraws. Purists among the guests will change into clean socks. At the designated time, which may be announced by the sounding of a gong, the guests leave all their belongings in the waiting room, wash their hands in a bowl provided for that purpose outside of the tearoom, then crawl into the room, leaving their shoes outside. They may enter the room in the order of seniority, determined by age, experience, or relationship to the tea master.

Each guest, after entering the tearoom, turns around and moves his shoes out of the way, arranging them neatly and pointed outward. Each guest then slowly and methodically goes to the *toko-no-ma* (toe-koe-no-mah), or alcove, to admire the hanging scroll there. After all have entered the room and admired the *toko-no-ma* display, they seat themselves before the brazier in order of seniority.

Conversation and comments are subdued and thoughtful, in keeping with the surroundings and purpose of the ceremony. The host enters and formally welcomes each guest, bowing to each of them. The guests return the bows. The host then lights incense sticks. Guests may inspect the incense box to admire its beauty.

If food is to be included in the ceremony it is served at this time. Guests inspect the food and serving ware carefully, and eat slowly, savoring the experience. When the meal is finished, the guests return to the waiting room while the host cleans the tearoom, exchanges the alcove scroll for a flower arrangement, and brings out the utensils to be used in the tea ceremony.

When these preparations are completed the guests are called in again. They admire the flower arrangement and the tea utensils before seating themselves. The host returns, ceremoniously prepares the tea, and then begins the service by passing the large tea bowl to the highest ranking guest.

The guest holds the tea bowl in his left hand, turns it twice clockwise with his right hand so the motif on the bowl faces the host, takes three and a half sips, sets the bowl down, wipes the edge of the bowl where he drank with a cloth provided for that purpose, rotates the bowl again so the motif is facing him, then passes it to the next guest.

After each guest has repeated this ceremony the tea bowl is passed back to the host who cleans it and hands it back to the guests to examine and admire. Bowls and other utensils used in the traditional ceremony are usually masterpieces of craftsmanship, often hundreds of years old, and are representative of what the Japanese call *shibui* (she-buu-ec) beauty—the epitome of simplicity, naturalness, and harmony.

All the other utensils used in the ceremony are again examined and discussed, each guest striving to merge with the spirit of the object. Afterward, the host may serve something sweet, accompanied by ordinary tea. This part of the ceremony is more casual, but still carefully orchestrated. At the appropriate time, the senior guest takes the lead in bowing to the host and thanking him for the ceremony. The other guests follow suit, and all leave.

The dedicated host may then prepare himself a final

cup of tea, and in silence and solitude, sip it slowly, savoring the atmosphere to the fullest.

Newcomers to the tea ceremony may question other guests on points of behavior before the ceremony begins, and should follow their lead during the ceremony. Each of the commercial *cha-no-yu* schools has its own literature describing its ceremony. If you attend a ceremony open to the public you will most likely receive a small printed guide on what to do during the ceremony.

23

The Apology

The Japanese are famous for apologizing. They apologize often and in a wide variety of situations. Indeed, *sumimasen* (sue-me-mah-sen), the word most commonly used to mean "I'm sorry," is also commonly used for "thank you." The subtleties of this overlapping usage go to the heart of traditional Japanese culture, which, as mentioned earlier, is based on the concept of *wa* (wah), or harmony.

This overwhelming need for harmony led the Japanese to a highly stylized and ambiguous use of language that was calculated not to give offense. But even when the language was used in an esoteric, poetic, and indirect manner, there was always the danger of rubbing someone the wrong way, so apologizing in advance, during, and after almost any conversation became a standard practice.

Following the prescribed forms of physical etiquette was vital in feudal Japan—from bowing to parents, teachers, or others in authority, to moving off a road and kowtowing when a clan lord and his procession passed. But adhering to a more demanding verbal etiquette was even more critical. In such a society where the slightest deviation from the highest standards of behavior could be a serious transgression, it was essential that the Japanese have a socially accepted mechanism to atone for real as well as imaginary slights.

This mechanism was the apology, which could take a variety of forms, ranging from the simple *sumimasen* to suicide by a ritualistic slicing open of the abdomen. Verbal apologies as well as some of the more drastic forms of apology are still a distinctive part of contemporary Japanese life.

On any given day when out and about in Japan, one can hear dozens of verbal apologies. Many of them may sound silly or inappropriate to the outsider. Politicians and businessmen whose behavior has "insulted" the public routinely resign as a form of apology. This action, however, lost a great deal of its impact because of several major scandals that occurred in the 1980s and resulted in the resignations of scores of top business and political leaders.

It is essential that foreign visitors and businessmen

be aware of the role of the apology in Japan and be able to use it. As with any deviation from social norms, Japanese are highly sensitive to a failure to apologize in any of the numerous daily instances when an apology is appropriate. While Japanese rationally accept the fact that non-Japanese cannot be expected to follow Japanese apology etiquette, they cannot prevent themselves from reacting emotionally when such breaches occur. This emotionalism colors their opinion of foreigners and their reactions to them.

If you are not thoroughly familiar with the Japanese language or culture, the best procedure is to use the expression *sumimasen* any time you feel an apology might possibly be called for. If an apology was not called for, the Japanese will just think you are exceptionally polite—a character trait they appreciate and are themselves required to constantly cultivate.

24

Appreciation

Expressing and demonstrating appreciation has traditionally been an integral part of the Japanese etiquette system. As with other elements of that system, however, its rules and prescriptions were carried far beyond the norms of accepted behavior in the West. In the Japanese system every action required a balancing reaction, as in the Oriental principle of ying and yang, in which opposing forces balance and bring about harmony.

Appreciation was the expected response for any favor, assistance, or positive recognition; it was also required for repaying debts that came to one naturally as a result of birth—debts to one's parents, to instructors, to the clan lord, to the emperor, to the gods.

Verbal expressions of appreciation and "thank you" bows were as common as expressions of apology (if not more common). Again, the golden rule was to maintain harmony at all levels by sustaining maximum goodwill and emotional satisfaction. Verbal expressions of appreciation were generally accompanied by bows, ranging from very light to medium, depending on the circumstances. The more important the situation, the more formal and deeper the bow.

Other Japanese terms for "thank you," *dōmo arigatō gozaimasu* (doe-moe ah-ree-gah-toe go-zye-mahss), *arigatō gozaimasu* (ah-ree-gah-toe go-zye-mahss), and *dōmo* (doe-moe) in descending order of politeness, are also among the most common expressions in Japanese.

It is customary to thank people twice for treating you to drinks or food—the first time on the occasion, and the second time when you next meet them (if no more than three weeks have elapsed).

Verbal expressions of appreciation, however, are too ephemeral (not to mention potentially insincere) to give the emotional satisfaction required to maintain harmony. Institutionalized gift-giving is a logical response to this need for more meaningful ways of demonstrating appreciation.

In today's Japan, all the traditional ways of expressing and demonstrating appreciation continue to flourish. The Japanese not only give gifts in appreciation of past favors and goodwill, they give gifts as payment in advance for future goodwill and favors—something which often strikes the Westerner as bribery and therefore unethical behavior. A careful analysis of this system, however, reveals an intimate understanding of human nature and a degree of common sense at work that may attain better and even fairer results than the "ethically" based Western approach.

In earlier times, people planning to entertain guests at a restaurant would customarily tip the employees a day or so in advance to make sure they got the best possible reception and service. Emulation of the Japanese custom of expressing and demonstrating appreciation before *and* after a favor is granted will allow the outsider to function more smoothly and effectively in the Japanese environment. One challenge for foreign visitors and businessmen is to be aware of the special occasions when something more than verbal thanks is required. One of the most important of these special occasions for businessmen is at the beginning of the new year. Between January third and the tenth or eleventh, most businessmen personally visit as many of their customers and suppliers as they can, thanking them for past patronage and asking them to continue doing business with them during the new year.

Visitors to Japan expecting to meet people outside of the travel industry should take along small courtesy gifts to hand out to anyone who befriends them. If you are going to meet people with whom you hope to develop long-term relationships, gifts more appropriate for the situation and level of people involved may be advisable.

25

Dating

Dating, as it is practiced in the West, did not appear in Japan until the 1950s. In feudal Japan the custom was to separate boys and girls at a fairly early age for education and training, and thereafter strictly limit social relations among teenagers of the opposite sex. Virtually all marriages were arranged.

Love, when it occurred, was looked upon as forbidden fruit, disruptive of the social order. Although it may sound odd, true love relationships were more likely to occur between adult male customers and women working as prostitutes in the inns and red-light districts that dotted the country. Such an environment was really the only one in which the couple could be, if only temporarily, free from social constraints.

With the abolition in 1945 of the feudal family system in which the father held absolute sway over family members, and the introduction of individual freedom to Japan for the first time in the history of the country, the stage was set for the development of personal relations that would lead to dating and love marriages.

The young Japanese of this era gradually began picking up dating customs from the hundreds of thousands of American and Allied soldiers serving in the military forces that occupied Japan from 1945 to 1952.

It wasn't until well into the 1950s, however, when single Japanese felt free enough to express themselves individually and were affluent enough to spend purely for entertainment, that dating started to become a significant part of the Japanese scene.

Age-old customs and attitudes continued to maintain sharp divisions between the adult male and female worlds in Japan, however, preventing large numbers of people from establishing personal relationships with the opposite sex. Japanese still have not been able to overcome all the barriers inherent in groupism, in particular their reluctance to establishing new friendships without third-party introductions. As a result, somewhere between twenty and thirty percent of young Japanese men and women still do not date and depend upon third parties to arrange marriages for them.

One difference in Japanese and Western dating practices is that most dating couples in Japan rendezvous at train stations, coffee shops, restaurants, and other public places instead of at home. Most Japanese apartments and homes are not large enough or private enough to serve as trysting places for lovers. For this same reason a large national network of small hotels and inns, known as "love hotels," has arisen to cater to Japanese couples seeking privacy.

Dating couples in Japan engage in the same activities couples do in the West—going to restaurants, night spots, theaters, beaches, and mountains, going on weekend drives, and so on. At the same time, public display of affection is significantly more restrained than it is in the West.

There are, however, small groups of very conspicuous young people in Tokyo and other cities who are notorious for their bizarre style of dress and public behavior. In the Japanese way, these unconventional youths almost always keep to groups that gather in specific areas of the cities, such as the renowned Harajuku and Roppongi districts in Tokyo. The youths themselves are something of a sightseeing attraction.

Historically the Japanese attitude toward Japanese and foreign mixed couples has been strongly negative. Japanese culture has been so group oriented and so exclusive it has been difficult for one group to accept any outsider into the fold, even if the person were Japanese. Accepting a non-Japanese was practically unthinkable.

This attitude has changed dramatically since the late 1940s, when foreign-Japanese dating became commonplace during the Allied Occupation and thousands of mixed marriages occurred annually. But most Japanese have not accepted mixed dating or mixed marriages as natural and remain opposed to them.

Tolerance of mixed liaisons is, however, growing slowly among the Japanese majority. And, an increasing number of internationalized Japanese even see mixed dating and mixed marriages as highly desirable, one of the avenues by which Japan can become truly international. These people are delighted when their sons and daughters marry non-Japanese.

Eligible singles meet in Japan much as they do in the West. Popular meeting places include schools, restaurants, pubs, swimming pools, tennis courts, beaches, mountains, and so on. Nevertheless, many more dating couples in Japan are brought together by professional dating bureaus or by superiors at the workplace.

Given the still-acute sensitivity of the average Japanese to seeing mixed couples in Japan, foreign visitors and residents are advised to behave in a conservative manner and to avoid overt overtures to members of the opposite sex in public. On the other hand, due to the more relaxed attitude concerning sexual liaisons, most foreigners in Japan have options not readily available in their home countries. The only overriding rule of etiquette here is to do as the Japanese do and to not call attention to yourself.

26

Weddings

Weddings in Japan may fol-
low Shinto, Buddhist, or Christian customs. The most
common, however, is the Shinto ceremony, which is now
chosen by some eighty percent of marrying couples. It
became popular after Emperor Taisho was wedded in
this type of ceremony in 1900.

The actual wedding ceremony, which is generally attended only by the families and close friends of the
couple, is simple and lasts about twenty to thirty
minutes. A Shinto priest consecrates the union. Usually the bride and groom enter the ceremony hall preceded by a Shinto shrine maiden. Behind them is the
go-between and his or her spouse, followed by the
groom's parents and immediate family and the bride's
parents and immediate family. The go-between, or
nakōdo (nah-koe-doe), traditionally was the one who
made the match between the young couple. Today, with
arranged marriages becoming less and less common, the
person who takes this part in the wedding is more like
the best man in the West.

In a pure Shinto ceremony both the bride and groom
usually wear traditional wedding kimono. The bride
wears an elaborate coiffure (nowadays a wig) called a

takashimada (tah-kah-she-mah-dah) and a white head-dress called a *tsuno-kakushi* (tsoo-no-kah-koo-she), literally, "horn hider." The name comes from the idea that jealousy turned women into angry demons with horns. This headdress served as a warning that it was best to "hide one's horns."

After the priest announces the union, all stand and bow. Then *sansan-kudo* (san-san-koo-doe) is performed. This consists of the bride and groom taking three sips each of saké from three different-sized cups and symbolizes their union. The couple then reads wedding vows from a scroll. An exchange of wedding rings may or may not follow, depending on the couple's wishes. Finally, a branch of the sacred *sakaki* (sah-kah-key) tree is offered to the gods and the members of the two families each sip a cup of saké, drinking it dry in three sips. This symbolizes the union of the families and marks the end of the ceremony.

Although the Shinto wedding ceremony is the most common, there are also Buddhist and Christian ceremonies as well as numerous variations on the traditional. I attended one rather unusual wedding in which the bride wore a kimono, the groom a tuxedo, the ceremony was Shinto, the couple marched into the hall to the refrain "Here comes the bride," and then cut their Western wedding cake with a samurai sword.

Receptions, unlike the actual marriage ceremony, are large events with anywhere from fifty to several hundred guests in attendance. It is virtually mandatory that both the bride and groom's co-workers, including one or more of their superiors, attend the reception. Popular places for receptions include international hotels, wedding halls, and large restaurants.

An invitation to a reception will probably include a reply postcard. You should write your name and address on this and indicate whether or not you will attend. Write a short congratulatory message and, if unable to attend, a short explanation.

It is customary to bring a cash gift to the reception. Close friends, however, can also give gifts in the Western fashion, but these should be mailed early enough to arrive two weeks before the wedding. The typical cash gift is currently about twenty thousand yen. This, of course, varies according to your relationship with the couple. It is best to ask Japanese friends for advice on how much to give.

The money, in crisp new notes, should be enclosed in a special envelope called *noshibukuro* (no-she-buu-kuu-roe). These red and white envelopes, which are sold at stationery stores and convenience stores, are tied with a square knot of gold and silver cords and bear the Chinese character for *kotobuki* (koe-toe-buu-kee), meaning "happiness." In one corner is a decoration called *noshi* (no-she), which gives the envelope its name. Originally this was an actual piece of dried abalone but today it is a paper decoration.

Keep in mind that the elaborateness of the envelope should correspond to the amount of money enclosed.

It is bad form to buy a very fancy envelope, no matter how pretty, and then enclose a lesser amount than the envelope suggests. Very fancy envelopes have curlicued gold and silver cords, and plum, bamboo, and pine decorations in addition to the *noshi*. These are suitable for amounts over fifty thousand yen. A suitable envelope for twenty thousand yen has flat gold and silver cords, a *noshi* decoration in the corner and no extra folds or decorations. Tables will be set up at the entrance to the reception hall and this is where you present the *noshibukuro*.

The usual attire for a ceremony or reception is black suit, white shirt, and white tie for men. Women wear either kimono or a Western-style dress. Invitations often say to dress casually, but don't take this seriously unless you want to stand out.

Usually, receptions are formal, structured affairs, with either a skilled acquaintance or a professional serving as the master of ceremony. Receptions may take many forms, with the three most common being a sit-down meal, a Chinese-style meal with about eight guests to a round table, or a buffet-style stand-up party.

After the newlyweds arrive to loud applause and often to the strains of the "Wedding March," the master of ceremonies introduces himself and the go-between. The go-between then makes a speech about the couple, and this is followed by a few more speeches by family members. The first few speeches are formal and complimentary. The tone is felicitous with no off-color jokes.

Finally, everyone stands for the toast and from here

on the atmosphere becomes a bit less formal. Next may come the cutting of the wedding cake. Then dinner is served, and the bride and groom will likely make a speech. Then the couple changes outfits. They may change as many as three times.

Afterward, friends of both the bride and groom take turns at the microphone, relating incidents from the past. These speeches are invariably lighter in tone, and often humorous or a bit embarrassing to the bride or groom. Congratulatory telegrams may also be read at this time. If called upon to give a speech, note that it is improper to include words such as "part," "leave," "return," or anything relating to separation or sadness.

Finally, one of the parents of either the bride or groom will pay his respects to the guests with a short speech. The bride and groom may then present their parents with bouquets. This marks the end of the reception. The newlyweds and family see the guests off at the door, where guests receive a gift, called *hikide-mono* (hee-key-day-mow-no), loosely translated as "parting gift."

27

Funerals

Most funerals in Japan are conducted according to Buddhist rites, with details varying according to the sect. A notice of mourning, written on a piece of white paper with a black frame, is posted on the front door or at the gate of the house throughout the mourning period.

The wake, *tsuya* (tsoo-yah), was originally observed throughout the night to mourn for the dead and to pray for the repose of his or her soul. Recently it has become customary to hold a "half" wake, which usually starts around 6 p.m. in winter and 7 p.m. in summer. It may last as late as 10 p.m. Incense sticks are burned and a Buddhist priest recites sutras. Mourners then take turns burning a pinch of incense. At the end of the wake, food, usually meatless dishes, and saké or tea and cookies, is served. The mourners bring "condolence money," *kōden* (koe-den), in a white envelope tied with black and white or silver and white strings. *Kōden* should be brought to the wake or the memorial service.

The day after the wake the funeral service is held at home or at the parish temple or funeral hall. In the most common Buddhist-style funeral, the altar is prepared with a tablet inscribed with the posthumous name and a picture of the deceased, candleholders, incense burners, flowers, and other Buddhist ritual implements. The family of the deceased sits on the right side and relatives and friends on the left, facing the altar. Other participants sit in the back. The funeral rites begin with the recitation of sutras by a Buddhist priest and conclude with family members and relatives burning pinches of incense in turn while the priest continues to recite. The priest and family of the deceased then move to the side of the altar to make room for other participants to come to the altar and pay their last respects by burning pinches of incense.

If the deceased was a close friend or business acquaintance, you will have to decide whether to attend the wake or the memorial service or both. If unable to attend either, you could send a telegram of condolence, *chōden* (choe-den) or *o-kuyami denpō* (oh-koo-yah-me den-poe), followed by condolence money. The condolence money should be placed in the proper envelope (described later) and mailed by registered mail with or without a letter of sympathy. If no letter is enclosed, the gift should be preceded by a condolence telegram.

Sending such a telegram is a simple matter in Japan. Samples of appropriate messages are found listed in the back of Japanese telephone directories. Simply dial 115 and ask to send a telegram. The operator will call back and you need only to quote the listed number of the desired message.

The condolence money should be enclosed in special envelopes called *busshūgi-bukuro* (boo-shoe-gee-boo-koo-roe), or *kōden-bukuro,* which are available at any stationery store and most convenience stores. The envelopes are tied with black and white or silver strings tied in a flat square knot, as for weddings. These knots symbolize eternity. The strings may be printed on the envelope. The envelopes are also imprinted with Chinese characters, the text depending on whether the funeral is Buddhist, Shinto, or Christian. The simplest method of choosing an envelope is to ask for the one marked *go-reizen* (go-ray-zen). This means "before the spirit of the departed" and is acceptable for any religion.

Inside the outer folded paper is another envelope. This is where you put the money. The amount varies depending on your relationship to the deceased as well as your age. Three or five thousand yen is usually appropriate if the deceased was someone you had never met or knew only fleetingly, perhaps a relative of a co-worker or acquaintance. Five thousand yen is the minimum for a friend or business acquaintance. Between ten and thirty thousand yen is the minimum if the deceased was a relative. It should also be noted that like the *noshibukuro* (no-she-boo-koo-roe) used for money gifts at weddings and festive occasions, the ornateness of the *kōden* envelope should be in keeping with the amount of money enclosed. An envelope with printed strings is correct for three or five thousand yen. Envelopes with actual black and white strings attached are appropriate for gifts of ten thousand.

Mark the inner envelope on front with the cash amount enclosed and write your name and address on the back of the inner envelope in the lower left corner. The name of the deceased is written down the center on the front of the outer envelope. Instructions for folding the envelope are usually included. It is the custom to bring the *kōden* with you if you attend the memorial service.

28

Attending a Wake

The correct attire for wakes and funeral services is more strictly adhered to in Japan than in the West. Men should wear black suits, with black necktie, socks, and shoes. Women should wear a black suit or dress, black stockings, and black shoes, and carry a black handbag. Make-up should be kept to a minimum and accessories in general are unacceptable. Anything shiny, such as patent leather or vinyl shoes or handbags is also taboo. However, wedding and engagement rings or simple pearl necklaces are permissible.

When called upon to attend a wake, there is often no time to return home from work and change. In this case it is acceptable for a man to attend in his regular work suit, but he should exchange his necktie for a black one. These are often sold at kiosks at train stations or in convenience stores. Women may also go directly from work if wearing a somber-colored dress or suit.

It is usual for only relatives and close friends of the deceased to attend a wake, but in the event that one wishes to attend, there are a few things to know. The first thing to do upon arriving is to pay your respects in front of the coffin. This is done by lighting incense sticks from either a standing or seated position.

After entering the room, bow to the family and move to the altar. Bow to the picture placed on the altar. Then, with your right hand, light an incense stick from the candle. If it flames up be sure to not *blow* the flame out. The flame should be extinguished by *fanning* it with your left hand. Set the stick in the incense holder and fold your hands in prayer, bowing your head. Bow again to the family and chief mourner.

When offering incense from a seated position the procedure is much the same. Bow from a kneeling position to the family. Then approach the altar, in front of which is a cushion. Kneel before the cushion and bow. Then move the cushion aside and kneel where it had been placed. Bow and light the incense. Fold your hands together in prayer again, then bow to the family again. Actually, most Japanese do not bother to move the cushion, but it is the correct etiquette.

If you wish, offer a word of condolence to the family. A good phrase to know is *go-shūshō-sama de gozaimasu* (go-shoe-show-sah-mah day go-zye-mahss), which is the equivalent of "you have my deepest sympathies." Then you should be seated. Friends are seated on the left of the room as you enter. The less close the relationship to the deceased, the further from the altar you should sit.

After lighting incense sticks, a priest may offer prayers lasting about thirty minutes. During this time, all attending may offer powdered incense in a ritual called *shōkō* (show-koe). This may either be done at the altar or if the incense burner is passed around the room, where one is sitting. This is almost the same procedure as with the incense stick except that the incense is in a powdered form. Take a pinch of incense and raise it to eye level while bowing slightly. Then place the incense in the censer (incense burner). Some people do this two or three times, but once is sufficient.

Following the prayer chantings, a light meal may be served. If you were not very close to the deceased, you should leave before the meal.

29

Attending a Funeral Service

This is the main service usually held the day following the wake and differs depending on the religion of the deceased.

Upon arriving at the funeral site, proceed to the reception table, offer a word of condolence, and sign your name in the book provided for that purpose. Then offer the *kōden,* the condolence money described earlier. You can add a simple phrase such as *go-reizen ni dōzo* (go-ray-zen knee doe-zoe), which roughly translates as "this is something for the departed."

At a Buddhist service, prayers are performed while you offer incense. If the prayers are to be made while standing, bow first to the family and chief mourner and proceed to the altar. Look at the picture and fold your hands together in prayer. Then move to the incense holder and bow before burning a pinch of incense.

In Shinto ceremonies, prayers are performed by offering the *tama-gushi* (tah-mah-goo-she), a branch from the *sakaki* (sah-kah-key) tree with white pieces of paper attached to it. You should take the branch offered by the priest and hold it in both hands with the stem pointing to yourself. Your right hand should support the stem as your left hand lightly supports the leafy end. Bow to the priest, then turn the *tama-gushi* ninety degrees counterclockwise so the leaves are pointing left. Advance to the altar and raise the branch to eye level once. Then, keeping it flat, turn the branch clockwise until the stem is pointing to the altar, and lay it on the table. Step back two or three steps, bow twice, and clap your hands silently twice. Again bow to the family and to the priest.

In a Christian ceremony in Japan, it is a custom for participants to place a single flower on a table in front of the coffin. After receiving a flower, bow to the family and proceed to the table placed before the coffin, holding the flower by resting the stem part on your left hand and the flower part on your right hand. The blossom should be pointed to your right. At the altar bow before the picture and turn the flower to the right so the blossom is now pointing toward you. You are still holding the stem with your left hand, the blossom with your right. Place the flower on the table alongside the others. Bow again to the altar and then once more to the family.

30

Temples and Shrines

Temples and shrines abound in Japan and distinguishing between the two is often a problem for foreigners. Temples are Buddhist and are called *o-tera* (oh-tay-rah); shrines are Shinto and are called *jinja* (jeen-jah).

Probably the most distinguishing feature of Shinto shrines is the *torii* (toe-ree), or "gate," that stands before all shrines and has long been symbolic of Japan. The *torii* consists of two upright pillars with two crossbeams at the top. The primary function of the *torii* is to mark the boundary of the shrine. It also signals visitors that they are inside sacred precincts and should behave accordingly. Generally, the larger the shrine the larger the *torii*. The more expansive the shrine grounds the more likely there will be two or more of these gates over the walkways leading up to the main shrine.

Also at the entrance to shrines one can often find a pair of "Korean dog" stone statues, called *koma-inu* (koe-mah-eeh-noo), one guarding either side of the entrance. They are slightly asymmetrical and one always has its mouth open, the other has its closed. They may also occasionally be found in front of temples, but in Japan they are generally associated with Shinto.

111

Within the shrine precincts, usually toward the rear, one will find the *haiden* (high-den), or main hall of worship. Other than the *haiden* there is the main sanctuary, or *honden* (hone-den), where the spirit of the shrine deity is believed to reside.

Near the *haiden* is a pavilion for rinsing your hands and mouth, called *te-mizu-ya* (tay-me-zoo-yah). This is a symbolic purification one is expected to perform before approaching the sanctuary or temple.

After going up to the main hall, you will see a heavy rope, under which is a wooden donation box, *saisen-bako* (sigh-sen-bah-koe). First throw your donation into the box. Then pull the rope that is attached to the eaves and rings a bell. This is to attract the attention of the shrine deity. Then clap your hands two or three times and bow your head, holding the bow for a few seconds. Do not clap your hands at a temple.

Both Shinto shrines and Buddhist temples can range in size from small, single buildings to large complexes with numerous buildings of varying sizes, in which may be held a variety of meetings and services. Sometimes the temples or shrines are little more than tiny shelters, in which the deities are enshrined.

The very large or famous shrines, such as Meiji Shrine in Tokyo, attract visitors from across the country. At these shrines, religious artifacts, good-luck charms, and ornaments are sold (technically they are exchanged for donations) at booths or other buildings on the grounds.

The etiquette when visiting the interior of a temple or shrine is the same as when visiting a private home in Japan, the main point being that you remove your shoes.

31

Obfuscation

Japanese are noted for not saying what they think, or expressing themselves subtly or obliquely, even in private. This is such an ingrained cultural trait that it has influenced both the structure and the use of the language. This behavior is, of course, part of the overall etiquette, in which the need for surface harmony takes precedence over other considerations and creating friction or irritation is considered taboo.

There are now many Japanese whose exposure to Western concepts and behavior has de-Japanized them to the point that they will speak directly and make specific commitments. But generally speaking they are able to do this only when acting privately on matters that concern them alone. In business situations where others are concerned, the Japanese are still compelled to go by the rules of the group, which dictate that decisions must be based on a broad consensus of lower, middle, and upper management.

Some Japanese "authorities" go so far as to claim that the way Japanese and Westerners think and behave is different because we do not use the left and right sides of our brains in the same way. They maintain that Japanese thinking is primarily based on intuition and the need for harmony, while Western thinking emphasizes intellect and logic. These two functions, they say, are handled by opposite sides of the brain.

True or not, the group orientation of Japanese society makes it virtually impossible for individuals to make unilateral statements or commitments for themselves or their groups, except when one is chosen to act as spokesman for the group after consensus has been reached and a decision formalized. Prior to this point, individual Japanese, even on the highest level, can only speak of hopes and possibilities. In fact, before consensus is reached, *nobody* in a Japanese company or organization really knows what the outcome of any discussion or negotiation will be. The more they are pressed for a response, the more vague and unresponsive they are likely to be. Pressure beyond a certain point can even result in a complete breakdown in communication.

Japanese obfuscation is *usually* not designed to maliciously mislead, delay, or cause problems. It is designed to maintain harmony while allowing the group approach to work.

There are naturally specific rules of etiquette for dealing with this obfuscation factor. This etiquette is based on avoiding direct confrontation, not putting anyone on the spot, and using third parties—insiders if possible—to give regular readings on the status of any ongoing negotiations or project planning. Sometimes these readings are accurate and helpful; at other times they may not be. There is always an element of uncertainty.

If you have a close personal relationship with an upper-level member of a Japanese group—for example a worker who is at the section-chief level or above—take him out for a drinking session. In this informal environment, you can often get a fairly good idea about whether your project is proceeding smoothly. The casual atmosphere and real or pretended state of inebriation enable him to level with you.

If you find yourself in a situation in which the intent or desire of a Japanese is unclear and you really need to know where you stand, your best recourse is to ask a mutual friend or a neutral go-between to find out what is going on.

32

Inns

Japan's *ryokan* (rio-kahn), or inns, which appeared in great numbers in the mid-1600s and have flourished ever since, are like time portals to the country's past. They have perpetuated the traditional culture that grew out of the court life that flowered in Kyoto from 794 to 1868 A.D. *Ryokan* make it possible for people today to enjoy the same highly refined lifestyles perfected by the members of the imperial family and the clan lords.

It is in the inns of Japan that one finds the epitome of Japanese aesthetics—the pliant reed-mat floors, the beautiful sliding door panels, the *toko-no-ma* altars, the exquisite tableware produced by master artisans, the sensual *yukata* robes, the stimulating hot baths, the traditional foods, and the kind and quality of service honed for centuries to elevate every guest to the level of royalty. It is in the traditional inns of Japan that the visitor can see and experience Japanese etiquette in its purest form.

Popular inns, particularly those outside of the major cities, are invariably located on sites of scenic beauty, often overlooking the sea, a river or lake, or a stunning, stream-carved gorge. Many sites are further enhanced by the subtle, natural beauty of Japanese landscaping.

Upon entering the *genkan* (gen-kahn), or foyer, of an inn, you are welcomed by kimono-clad maids. You remove your shoes in the foyer, step up to the inn floor and don slippers, to be used in the hallway and public areas. After being guided to your room, which is oriented to take the fullest possible advantage of the scenic view, you are directed to exchange your street clothes for *yukata,* then provided with tea and usually a snack such as fruit or tiny cubes of bean jam. This begins a totally Japanese experience that will allow you to employ many of the rules of etiquette previously discussed, from sitting and eating on the floor to bathing.

All meals and drinks are served in your room, unless you are with a group that is served communal meals in a large dining area. When you want service you use an interphone or push a call button. Toilets are usually located outside of the rooms, and in many places the commodes will be elongated ceramic bowls, at floor level, that flush. Keep in mind that the hallway and public area slippers are never worn into the rooms or the toilets. You leave your slippers outside the toilet door, donning others on the inside. When you see slippers outside of a toilet you know it is occupied.

Your *yukata* may also be worn outside of the inn, for walks or shopping excursions, even for playing golf. There is, of course, a right way and a wrong way to wear the *yukata*. The left side should be wrapped over the right side. Right-over-left wrapping is reserved for the dead. Men wrap the *yukata* sash (belt) low around their hips and tie it on the right side. Women wrap the sash around their waists and tie it in the back.

If it is rainy, the inn will provide you with an umbrella, often a traditionally styled one made of colorful paper. Make a note to find out if your inn has a *mongen* (moan-gen), or "closing time," when the front door is locked. If it does and you plan on being out after that time, make sure you know where the entry doorbell is located.

33

Saying Farewell

Many people are familiar with the Japanese expression *sayonara,* or "goodbye." But few are aware of its literal meaning, "if it must be so"—a very lyrical and emotional way of expressing the sense of loss and sadness often felt when parting.

Unfortunately, the Japanese habit of incorporating foreign words into their language has significantly reduced the use of *sayonara,* particularly among young people who prefer the exotic appeal of "bye-bye." This U.S. baby talk was introduced into Japan by American military personnel during the Occupation. The GIs used the expression with their Japanese girlfriends because it was much easier for the girls to say than "goodbye" (which usually comes out "guu-duu-bye" when pronounced by Japanese).

Japanese mothers now teach their infants "bye-bye" instead of "sayonara." Young Japanese schoolgirls, in particular, engage in a prolonged ritual of waving and saying "bye-bye" to each other when they part for the day, continuing until their friends are out of sight.

As Japanese girls and boys become adults, however, they use "bye-bye" less frequently, changing to the more traditional forms of farewell, including "sayonara." One conspicuous exception to this are Japan's thousands of cabaret hostesses who continue saying "bye-bye" to their male guests because it helps them maintain a deliberately infantile demeanor that is pleasurable to the men. The more formal the occasion, the more likely the farewell will include bowing, followed by hand-waving (the hand is waved from side to side and not up-and-down, which is the Japanese way of beckoning).

The most conspicuous of Japan's farewell customs is the ceremonial shout of "Banzai!" accompanied by raised arms. "Banzai" is short for "may you live 10,000 years," and was once primarily used as a salute to the emperor and as the equivalent of "Charge!" by samurai and the military.

The term is still used today in the original way as well as to commemorate special events such as the beginning or completion of some task or meeting, when newlyweds leave on their honeymoons, when businessmen leave for new posts, when groups of businessmen or politicians go abroad on missions, and so on. In these situations it is very much like "Hip! Hip! Hooray!"

On formal and semiformal occasions there is usually a leader who "conducts" the shouting of "banzai" and the arm raising to make sure it is done in unison. One may see groups of people at train stations and airports shouting *banzai* to their departing friends and colleagues in what appears to be a well-rehearsed and practiced ceremony.

Set phrases to be used upon leaving and returning

home, for whatever purpose or length of time, have also been formalized. When one leaves the home it is customary to call out to those remaining behind *itte kimasu* (eat-tay kee-mahss) or the more polite and humble *itte mairimasu* (eat-tay my-ree-mahss), both of which literally mean "I am going and coming." The practical English equivalent is "I'll be back."

In earlier times one stood in the *genkan*, or entrance foyer, faced the inside of the house, bowed, and said one of the above stock phrases. Nowadays they are said very casually and without bowing (except perhaps by sticklers for old-fashioned etiquette). The proper response by those remaining at home is *itte irasshai* (eat-tay ee-rah-shy), literally meaning "please go and come," and which functions like the English "see you later."

Upon returning home one calls out *tadaima* (tah-dah-ee-mah), which literally means "just now" but practically means "I'm home." The proper response to this is *o-kaerinasai* (oh-kye-ree-nah-sigh), literally "return" and functioning like our "welcome home."

It is also fairly common for people working in offices or shops to use these terms when going on errands or making other brief trips.

Other conventionalized expressions used when bidding someone farewell are:

O-genki de (oh-gen-kee day). This means something like "go in good health," and is said to someone who is leaving for an extended trip. It is particularly used when it is uncertain if and when you will see the people again, or when their health is of concern.

Ki o tsukete (kee oh tsoo-kay-tay). This expression means "be careful" or "take care" and is said to children, older people, or anyone who might face some kind of danger while out or traveling.

Ganbatte (gahn-baht-tay). Roughly translated "hang in there" or "don't give up," this is often called out to those engaged in competition or some difficult task, or to those about to embark on some demanding undertaking. The present tense of the verb, *ganbarimasu* (gahn-bah-ree-mahss), "I will try my best," is one of the most commonly used expressions in the language.

Glossary of Etiquette Terms

Baishaku (by-shah-kuu). Proper etiquette in preparing for an arranged marriage is to engage the services of a *baishaku*, or "go-between," who may be a relative, friend, or a professional. *Baishaku* is a formal term for go-between. The more common term is *nakōdo* (nah-koe-doe). A marriage arranged by a go-between is called a *baishaku kekkon* (by-shah-kuu keck-kone), or "go-between marriage."

Banzai (bahn-zye). This is a traditional exclamation shouted as an expression of joy upon some festive occasion, or as a rallying cry before some demanding action. It is shouted three times. Each time the arms are raised over the head with the hands outstretched. When "Banzai!" is the appropriate cheer, there is usually a leader who cues the group so that they all shout in unison.

Dōmo (doe-moe). This is the "very" and "much" part of "thank you very much." It also has the meaning of "really." It is used colloquially as "thanks" in very informal situations as well as "thank you" in more formal situations. Like *sumimasen* (sue-me-mah-sen), it is also used to express the idea of "excuse me" or "sorry" when relatively light apologies are called for. This is another of the most commonly used words in the language.

Dōmo arigatō (doe-moe ah-ree-gah-toe). This is equivalent to "thank you." It is mostly said to co-workers, friends, and to tradespeople.

Dōmo arigatō gozaimashita (doe-moe ah-ree-gah-toe go-zye-mahssh-tah). This is the past tense of "thank you very much," and it is used after something has been done for which you should express appreciation. Since this may be only seconds after the event, its use sometimes appears to overlap its present tense form.

Dōmo arigatō gozaimasu (doe-moe ah-ree-gah-toe go-zye-mahss). This is the equivalent of "thank you very much," used to express appreciation for something that is being done for you at that time, or will be done in the future (as when someone offers to perform some favor). The expression is very polite and it is common for the person saying it to bow slightly when using it.

Go-chisō-sama deshita (go-chee-so-sah-mah desh-tah). This expression is used after one has been treated to drinks and or food by someone. It may also be said upon leaving a restaurant, bar, etc. It roughly translates as "thank you very much for the food/drinks."

Go-kurō-sama (go-kuu-roe-sah-mah). *Kurō* by itself means "hardship" or "trouble." *Go* is an honorific prefix. This expression is said to people, often employees, after a day's work or upon the completion of a task. The Japanese are sensitive about such recognition and use this expression often. It should be noted that this expression is usually used with people from whom the work is, although appreciated, nonetheless expected. See *O-tsukare-sama deshita*.

Itadakimasu (ee-tah-dah-kee-mahss). This is used prior to eating or drinking when you are with someone, particularly if you are a guest, and also if there is no designated or understood host. The original meaning of the word is "receive" or "accept." Its use serves notice that you are going to start eating. If you are a guest, it also acknowledges the fact that you are receiving something from the host. In a relatively small, more formal setting, the guests often do not start eating or drinking until the host gives a sign—usually by saying *dōzo* (doe-zoe), which in this case means "please (start, go ahead)." The guests then say *itadakimasu* and start.

Itadakimashita (ee-tah-dah-kee-mahss-tah). The past tense of the above word, *itadakimashita* is a polite way of saying "I have eaten/drunk it" or "I already have a helping/drink."

Kanreki (kahn-ray-kee). This is the celebration marking the sixtieth birthday, in the Orient considered an important milestone in life. Its observation comes from the fact that the old calendar system was based on a cycle of sixty years. Living to be sixty was an important achievement because it meant you had completed one full cycle of life and figuratively had been reborn as a baby. A popular present on this day was a red sleeveless kimono of the type traditionally worn by babies. It was also popularly held that once men and women reached this age they could ignore etiquette and responsibility and act like a baby again.

Kekkon hirō-en (keck-kone he-roe-en). This is the wedding banquet held after a wedding to officially announce the marriage to relatives and friends.

Miai kekkon (me-eye keck-kone). This is an arranged marriage. *Mi* means "see" and *ai* means "come together." *Ai* is also the pronunciation of the word for love, so one could also imagine that love has developed from the initial meetings.

O-jama shimasu (oh-jah-mah she-mahss). *Jama* means a hindrance, disturbance, or nuisance. When used in this sentence it means "I am going to disturb you." It is said when entering someone's home or office (after being invited in).

O-jama shimashita (oh-jah-mah she-mahssh-tah). The past tense of *o-jama shimasu,* this phrase is said when leaving someone's home or office after a visit. It means "I have disturbed you."

O-kaeshi (oh-kye-she). Receiving a gift makes a return gift, called *o-kaeshi,* mandatory. The return gift does not have to be as elaborate or as expensive as the gift received, particularly if there was a special reason for the person giving the gift and it is quite valuable. The *o-kaeshi* is usually just enough to acknowledge the gift you received and convey your appreciation.

O-kage-sama de (oh-kah-gay-sah-mah day). In their efforts not to accept responsibility or take credit, the Japanese have developed a number of expressions to share any credit that might be due. The term *o-kage-sama de,* something like "thanks to you," is used to give the other person credit for the speaker's health or success. If you ask someone how they are, a common response is *o-kage-sama de, genki desu* (oh-kah-gay-sah-mah day, gen-kee dess), or "thanks to you, I'm fine."

O-kyaku-san (oh-kyack-sahn). *O-kyaku-san,* or "Honorable guest," is a useful term that allows you to address visitors or guests in a respectful way without knowing their names or social standing. In status-conscious, insult-sensitive Japan, the term gets a considerable amount of use.

O-machidō-sama deshita (oh-mah-chee-doe-sah-mah desh-tah). It means "I'm sorry I kept you waiting."

O-saki ni, shitsurei shimasu (oh-sah-kee nee she-tsoo-ray she-mahss). Proper etiquette calls for those leaving work first to inform or advise their co-workers with the set expression *o-saki ni,* meaning, more or less, "I'm going first." *Shitsurei shimasu* means "I'm being rude," so together these mean something like "excuse me for being rude and leaving ahead of you." Leaving without saying anything may be regarded as uncaring.

O-somatsu-sama (oh-soe-maht-sue-sah-mah). This is used by wives or other hosts after being thanked by guests for a meal. The guests will normally say *go-chisō-sama* (see above); the host responds with *o-somatsu-sama,* which means more or less "it was nothing elaborate."

O-tsukare-sama deshita (oh-tsoo-kah-ray-sah-mah desh-tah). The root verb *tsukareru* (tsoo-kah-ray-rue) means "to become tired." It is used in the above form as a combination farewell and an expression of thanks at the close of a long day of hard work. It is a thoughtful and proper thing to say to anyone who works beyond normal hours or especially hard.

Sansan-kudo (sahn-sahn-kuu-doe). This means three times three equals nine, and refers to the three sips that are taken from three saké cups by the bride and groom, part of the nuptial oath in the Shinto wedding ceremony. Three is regarded as a lucky number in Japan, with three times three resulting in nine or a "great number," which symbolizes the strength of the wedding vows.

Senbetsu (sen-bet-sue). Custom calls for relatives and friends to give parting gifts, or *senbetsu,* to those leaving on trips, especially when the trips involve lengthy periods abroad. In earlier days, these were actually gift items. Nowadays, however, *senbetsu* almost always refers to a cash gift, and the trip doesn't have to be particularly long. Of course, the traveler is expected to bring something back for the gift giver.

Shitsurei shimasu (she-tsoo-ray she-mahss). The noun *shitsurei* means "a breach of etiquette, a discourtesy." *Shitsurei shimasu* means "I am being (or am about to be) impolite or rude." This can be said when you walk in front of someone, when you are about to leave someone or a group, when you are in the process of slightly disturbing or inconveniencing someone (as when reaching across in front of them or when carrying a large box and squeezing by them, etc.).

Shitsurei shimashita (she-tsoo-ray she-mahssh-tah). The past tense of *shitsurei shimasu,* this is used in the sense of "excuse me" or "pardon me" after you have bumped into someone or otherwise disturbed or inconvenienced them. Such inconveniences include giving out wrong information or being wrong about something even if it is relatively unimportant.

Sumimasen (sue-me-mah-sen). The original meaning of this expression is "it never ends." It is now used to mean "excuse me" or "pardon me," and also "I'm sorry" and "thank you." It is the most common way of calling out to get the attention of a waiter, waitress, or clerk, and also the most common expression for on-the-spot apologies for trivial transgressions. Along with *dōmo* (see above) it is one of the most commonly used words in the language.

Sumimasen deshita (sue-me-mah-sen desh-tah). The past tense of *sumimasen* is used as an apology for something that occurred earlier.

Te-uchi (tay-oo-chee). This is a rhythmic hand-clapping ceremony that is used in Japan to mark the closing of important parties or receptions and the consummation of alliances and business agreements. The hands are usually clapped ten times, in sets of three followed by a single clap. This cycle is then repeated three times.

Yaku-doshi (yah-kuu-doe-she). In Japan certain ages are

regarded as very unlucky for men (twenty-five and forty-two) and for women (nineteen and thirty-three). Some people take this belief seriously and it is bad form to joke about it. In fact, some make a point of visiting shrines or temples to pray in hopes of warding off bad luck.

Yubi-kiri (yuu-bee-kee-ree). The literal translation of *yubi-kiri* is "finger cutting," referring to the somewhat gruesome custom of cutting off the tip of one's little finger to emphasize a promise or to apologize for a serious transgression. Now it refers to two people hooking their little fingers together and tugging slightly to symbolize a promise they have made with each other. It is common among children, and also between women, especially in the entertainment trades, and their male customers who make playful promises to each other. Japan's gangsters, the *yakuza* (yah-kuu-zah), still adhere to the original meaning of the term, and it is common to see members of this group with the tips of their little fingers missing.

Yui-nō (yuu-ee-no). These are betrothal gifts that are ceremoniously exchanged between the families of prospective brides and grooms. In earlier years these gifts were usually items such as saké and sea bream, considered auspicious. Today they are more likely to be money wrapped in fine paper and tied with silver and gold cords.

Za-rei (zah-ray). If you want to surprise the Japanese with your knowledge of traditional Japanese etiquette, do the *za-rei*, which means more or less "sitting bow." It is the formal bow made when sitting on a *tatami* reed-mat floor. To accomplish the bow, place the three large fingers of each hand on the floor in front of you, and bow forward from the waist. Your little finger and thumb should be joined in a circle.

Other Titles of Interest from Tuttle and Periplus

Japanese Etiquette: An Introduction
by the World Fellowship of the Tokyo Y.W.C.A
ISBN 0 8048 0290 4

Japanese Etiquette Today: A Guide to Business & Social Customs
by James M. Vardaman, Jr. & Michiko Sasaki Vardaman
ISBN 0 8048 1933 5

Essential Japanese Phrase Book
ISBN 962 593 804 4

Japanese for All Occasions
The Right Word at the Right Time
by Anne Kaneko
ISBN 0 8048 1567 4

Survival Japanese
How to Communicate without Fuss or Fear – Instantly!
by Boye De Mente
ISBN 0 8048 1681 6

Making Out in Japanese
by Todd & Erika Geers
ISBN 4 900737 09 7

Japanese for Fun
by Taeko Kamiya
ISBN 0 8048 1628 X

Easy Japanese
A Direct Approach to Immediate Conversation
by Samuel E. Martin
ISBN 0 8048 0157 6

Basic Japanese Conversation Dictionary
by Samuel E. Martin
ISBN 0 8048 0057 X

Instant Japanese
Everything You need in 100 Key Words
by Boye De Mente
ISBN 4 900737 07 0

Let's Study Japanese
by Jun Maeda
ISBN 0 8048 0362 5

Martin's Pocket English-Japanese/Japanese-English Dictionary
(all romanised)
by Samuel E. Martin
ISBN 0 8048 1588 7

All Romanised English-Japanese Dictionary
by Hyojun Romaji Kai
ISBN 0 8048 3306 0

Using Japanese Slang
by Ann Kasschau & Susumu Eguchi
ISBN 4 900737 36 4

Japanese Slang Uncensored
by Peter Constantine
ISBN 4 900737 03 8

Outrageous Japanese
Slang, Curses, and Epithets
by Jack Seward
ISBN 0 8048 1694 8